# Contents

# Preface

The main purpose of this book in its revised edition remains unchanged: to show how various kinds of writing activities, both guided exercises to develop particular skills and communication tasks involving free expression, can be built up into a coherent writing programme. Through such a programme it is intended that the learners should not only make *systematic* progress, through their growing mastery of the written language, but also see how writing is used for the purpose of *communication*.

The book has been extensively revised to ensure that it reflects current methodological practice. Integrated skills, highlighted even in the first edition, now have a chapter of their own. The number of examples has been expanded throughout, so that the book can be used for resource material. In particular, the activities in the *Writing for fun* sections should prove a useful and flexible addition for any teaching situation. Correcting written work and teaching handwriting have now been expanded into chapters, and there is a completely new chapter on teaching children.

The substance of this book is based on teacher-training courses, seminars and lectures given over the last fifteen years. A series of seminars on teaching writing which I had to give in Latin America in the early seventies set me thinking about the subject, while the interest and encouragement of the students of 'Course 317' on 'Composition' which I taught at Concordia University, Montreal, in 1976, obliged me to give my views on teaching writing a little more cohesion and coherence. However, a spell back in the classroom, with adolescents and children, made me appreciate once again what every teacher knows: that it is not enough to do the 'right' things. The 'writing for fun' activities came directly out of that experience.

# 1

# The nature and purpose of writing

## 1.1 What is writing?

When we write, we use *graphic symbols*: that is, letters or combinations of letters which relate to the sounds we make when we speak. On one level, then, writing can be said to be the act of forming these symbols: making marks on a flat surface of some kind. But writing is clearly much more than the production of graphic symbols, just as speech is more than the production of sounds. The symbols have to be arranged, according to certain conventions, to form words, and words have to be arranged to form sentences, although again we can be said to be 'writing' if we are merely making lists of words, as in inventories of items such as shopping lists.

As a rule, however, we do not write just one sentence or even a number of *unrelated* sentences. We produce *a sequence of sentences arranged in a particular order and linked together in certain ways*. The sequence may be very short — perhaps only two or three sentences — but, because of the way the sentences have been put in order and linked together, they form a coherent whole. They form what we may call a 'text'.

Not a great deal is known about individual methods of composing a text, but most people — professional writers among them — would agree that it is usually neither an easy nor a spontaneous activity. Sometimes writing comes easily, if we are in the right 'mood' or have a clear and perhaps pressing need to express something, but as a rule it requires some conscious mental effort: we 'think out' our sentences and consider various ways of combining and arranging them. We reread what we have written as a stimulus to further writing. Other common practices are making notes, drafting and revising. We may even write several versions of a text before we are satisfied with the result. Notice, for example, how the writer corrected and modified his draft of the text on page 2.

The reason for this is that we are *writing for a reader*. Writing involves the *encoding* of a message of some kind: that is, we translate our thoughts into language. Reading involves the decoding or interpretation of this message. But, except on those occasions when we are writing for ourselves — our shopping list may have been for this purpose — the reader is someone who is not physically present. This, after all, is why we normally choose this particular channel of communication rather than the more common one of speech. And because our reader is not present, and in some cases may not even be known to us, we have to ensure that what we write can be understood without any further help from us. This is the reason for the care we have to take with writing. It is by the organisation of our sentences into a text, into a coherent whole which is as explicit as possible and complete in itself, that we are able (or *hope* to be able) to communicate successfully with our reader through the medium of writing.

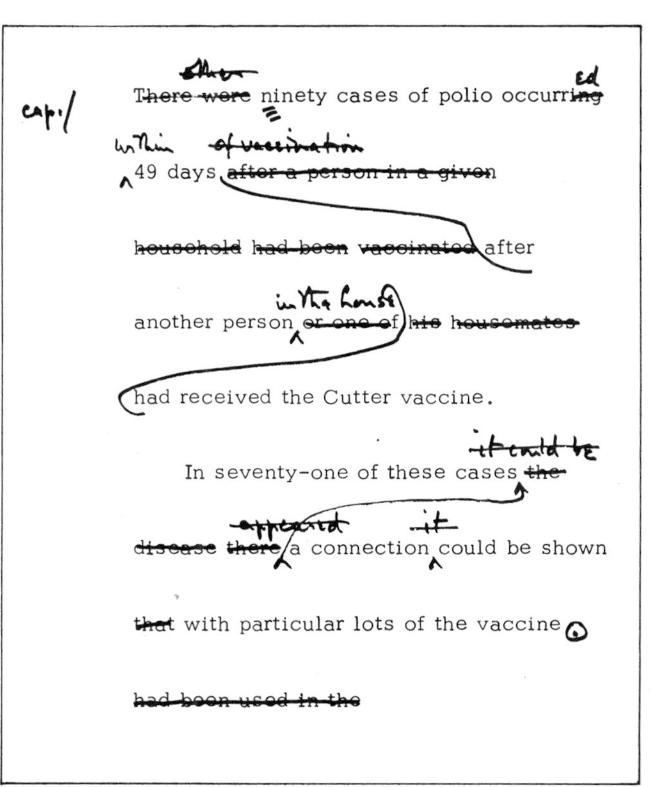
There were ninety cases of polio occurring
49 days after a person in a given
household had been vaccinated after
another person or one of his housemates
had received the Cutter vaccine.
In seventy-one of these cases the
disease there a connection could be shown
that with particular lots of the vaccine
had been used in the

## 1.2 What do we write?

It is helpful to keep in mind some of the many uses we are likely to make of writing. For example, on a personal level, most of us use writing to make a note of something (things we have to do or want others to do, like our shopping list), and to keep records of things we want to remember. We send messages and write letters to friends, and a few of us keep diaries. Most of us have to fill in forms from time to time (especially applications — for example, for insurance — or questionnaires) and occasionally we write formal letters (for example, if we change our job). Apart from this, the amount of writing we do regularly will relate to our professional life. Some might spend a good deal of time writing letters, instructions, reports, etc. For others this will only be an occasional activity.

Few of us, on the other hand, are likely to spend any time writing poetry or fiction. And, outside the classroom, we never write 'compositions' (*My daily routine*, *My favourite pastime*, etc.) of the kind that are still a feature of many examinations!

## 1.3 Speech and writing

A comparison between speech and writing should help us to understand some of the difficulties we experience when we write. The table on the next page highlights the main differences. Note, however, that it does not take into account certain situations in which the spoken language is used, such as telephoning and lecturing.

Although writing is clearly much more dependent on how effectively we use the linguistic resources of the language (see 1.4.2), it would be wrong to conclude that all the advantages are on the side of speech. While it is true that in writing we have the task of organising our sentences carefully so as to make our meaning as explicit as possible without the help of feedback from the reader, on the other hand we do not normally have to write quickly: we can rewrite and revise our sentences until we are satisfied that we have expressed our meaning. Equally, the reader is in a more privileged position than the listener to some extent: he can read at his own pace and reread as often as he likes. In this way, then, some of the disadvantages of communicating through the written medium are offset.

| SPEECH | WRITING |
|---|---|
| 1 Takes place in a *context*, which often makes references clear (e.g. '*that* thing over *there*') | 1 Creates its own context and therefore has to be fully explicit |
| 2 Speaker and listener(s) in contact. Interact and exchange roles | 2 Reader not present and no interaction possible |
| 3 Usually person addressed is specific | 3 Reader not necessarily known to writer |
| 4 Immediate feedback given and expected (a) verbal: questions, comments ... murmurs, grunts (b) non-verbal: facial expressions | 4 No immediate feedback possible. Writer may try to anticipate reader's reactions and incorporate them into text |
| 5 Speech is transitory. Intended to be understood immediately. If not, listener expected to interact | 5 Writing is permanent. Can be reread as often as necessary and at own speed |
| 6 Sentences often incomplete and sometimes ungrammatical. Hesitations and pauses common and usually some redundancy and repetition | 6 Sentences expected to be carefully constructed, and linked and organised to form a text |
| 7 Range of devices (stress, intonation, pitch, speed) to help convey meaning. Facial expressions, body movements and gestures also used for this purpose | 7 Devices to help convey meaning are punctuation, capitals and underlining (for emphasis). Sentence boundaries clearly indicated |

## 1.4 Why writing is difficult

We can now begin to understand why writing is a difficult activity for most people, both in the mother tongue and in a foreign language. We shall look at the problems which are caused by writing under three headings — psychological, linguistic and cognitive — although these inevitably overlap to some extent.

### 1.4.1 Psychological problems

Speech is the natural and normal medium of communication for us in most circumstances and accustoms us both to having someone physically present when we use language and to getting feedback of some kind. Writing, on the other hand, is essentially a solitary activity and the fact that we are required to write on our own, without the possibility of interaction or the benefit of feedback, in itself makes the act of writing difficult.

### 1.4.2 Linguistic problems

Oral communication is sustained through a process of interaction and, except in special circumstances, such as a lecture, the participants help to keep it going. Because speech is normally spontaneous, we have little time to pay attention either to organising our sentence structure or to connecting our sentences: to some extent the latter is maintained through the process of interaction. We repeat, backtrack, expand and so on, depending on how people react to what we say. Incomplete and even ungrammatical utterances usually pass unnoticed. Some of these features are illustrated in the sample of conversation which has been transcribed below:

DF: Pete, you composed this piece at the piano. Is that how you normally work?

PW: Always. Up to this point, always. It may be that might change in the future, when I get more into, you know, working from scratch with synthesisers, but at the moment I do write at the piano. Actually I didn't . . . I hardly realised I'd written this until I had! (*Laughs.*) One of those things that just dropped out of the sky!

DF: Well, how did you start, then?

PW: Er, well, we decided on a, erm, a sort of musical flavour that we should adopt for, for this particular number, and, erm, just followed where my fingers took me, really, you know. Er, we . . . I, I had an intro I'd . . . I was just noodling and doodling at the piano with this . . . (*sound of piano*)

As we have seen, we also have a considerable range of devices at our disposal to help get our meaning across. In writing, we have to compensate for the absence of these features: we have to keep the channel of communication open through our own efforts and to ensure, both through our choice of sentence structure and by the way our sentences are linked together and sequenced, that the text we produce can be interpreted on its own.

### 1.4.3 Cognitive problems

We grow up learning to speak and in normal circumstances spend much of our time doing it. We also appear to speak without much conscious effort or thought and generally we talk because we want to, about matters which are of interest or relevant to us socially or professionally. *Writing*, on the other hand, *is learned through a process of instruction*: we have to master the written form of the language and to learn certain structures which are less used in speech, or perhaps not used at all, but which are important for effective communication in writing. We also have to learn how to organise our ideas in such a way that they can be understood by a reader who is not present and perhaps by a reader who is not known to us.

Finally, writing is a task which is often imposed on us, perhaps by circumstances. This not only has a psychological effect; it may also cause a problem in terms of content — what to say. Being at a loss for ideas is a familiar experience to most of us when we are *obliged* to write.

## 1.5 Learning to write: mother tongue and foreign language situations compared

So far we have looked at writing in general, without drawing any distinction between writing in the mother tongue and writing in a foreign language. Clearly, however, there are important differences, particularly in the learning situation, and attention is now drawn to these.

Most children learn to write in their mother tongue at school, generally between the ages of five and seven. By this time they have a well-developed command of the spoken language, adequate at least to their social needs, but their experience of the written language is still very limited. Most children will of course have been exposed to it to some degree through being read to aloud. Writing itself, however, is a totally new experience for most of them.

Most children acquire this new skill fairly laboriously. On the other hand, they are required to make regular use of it, both in classes devoted to writing practice and, as their education progresses, in other lessons (history, geography, etc.) which involve some form of related and purposeful written work. Certain types of writing, particularly those which involve projection into adult-type roles, tend to cause them difficulty. Many children, in fact, simply do not enjoy writing, partly because of the nature of the task and partly because, out of school, it has little value for them as a form of social interaction, although in most cultures the ability to write carries prestige. Very few children succeed in becoming really proficient at writing and many cease to use this skill once they leave school, or use it only occasionally for specialised purposes (e.g. filling in forms).

In the light of this, we should, as foreign language teachers, be able to make certain assumptions, subject of course to cultural variations, and to avoid making others. Most of our students will already be familiar with the process of writing, unless they are very young, in which case writing will not — and should not — figure very prominently in the foreign language programme. They may have to learn a new script but writing itself will not be a new experience for them. They are also likely to have had a fairly wide experience of written language through reading in their mother tongue. They may also be at an age when they can learn through reading and perhaps the written language has come to have some psychological value for them as a form of support when learning something new.

We should not assume, however, that they are proficient at writing in their mother tongue, or that they already possess the necessary organisational skills for writing effectively. Nor should we assume that the ability to write in the mother tongue can be transferred to the foreign language, although some global transfer, as with reading ability, often seems to take place (that is, people who are highly literate in their own language easily become literate in another). It is also possible that the students' previous experience of learning to write and of practising writing in their own language was frustrating or unrewarding. As for their attitudes towards learning to write in a foreign language, we are rarely in a position to make any assumptions at all: these may range from no interest at all to a firm belief in its value to them as learners.

One very significant factor which affects writing in the foreign language classroom is that, even if we delay the introduction of writing for some time (see 4.1), the *amount* of language which the learners will have at their disposal for writing will be very limited — so limited that it might seem to make it impossible to introduce any meaningful form of writing practice. At the same time, the learners, being more mature than they were when they learned to write in their mother tongue, are conscious of the limitations which the foreign language imposes on the expression of their ideas. To resolve this problem it will be necessary to strike some sort of balance which prevents them from going beyond their linguistic attainment in the foreign language and yet will still provide them with writing activities which satisfy them on an intellectual level.

## 1.6 Why teach writing?

Clearly it is possible to learn to speak a foreign language without learning how to write in it and for many of our students, perhaps even the majority of them, writing will be the skill in which they are not only least proficient, even after considerable practice, but also the one for which they will have the least use. The situation is not so very different in the mother tongue, as we have already seen, except for those of us who use writing in some professional capacity. Because, therefore, writing is a skill which is both limited in value and difficult to acquire, we should be very clear about our purpose in teaching it.

In the *early stages* of a course oriented towards oral proficiency, writing serves a variety of *pedagogical* purposes:

(a) The introduction and practice of some form of writing enables us to provide for different learning styles and needs. Some learners, especially those who do not learn easily through oral practice alone, feel more secure if they are allowed to read and write in the language. For such students, writing is likely to be an aid to retention, if only because they feel more at ease and relaxed.

(b) Written work serves to provide the learners with some tangible evidence that they are making progress in the language. It is not likely to be a true index of their attainment, but once again it satisfies a psychological need.

(c) Exposure to the foreign language through more than one medium, especially if skills are properly integrated, appears to be more effective than relying on a single medium alone. Even at an elementary level there are many opportunities for activities that effectively integrate skills.

(d) Writing provides variety in classroom activities, serving as a break from oral work (and is therefore a quieter and more relaxed time for both students and teacher!). At the same time, it increases the amount of language contact through work that can be set out of class.

(e) Writing is often needed for formal and informal testing. Although in general oral ability should be measured through oral tests, in practice we are often obliged by circumstances, such as the amount of time we have at our disposal and the number of students there are in the class, to use some form of written test. In some cases, of course, a written test may even be appropriate: for example, making notes while listening.

These considerations strongly suggest that, while we should still concentrate on aural-oral skills in the early stages, we can make good use of writing, as part of an integrated skills approach to language learning. Although at this stage writing activities will be largely *a reinforcement of language learned orally**, this need not imply that writing has to be an unsatisfying or even rigidly controlled activity (see 3.3). It can also be taught in such a way that it prepares the learners for more realistic forms of writing at a later stage.

As the learners progress to the *intermediate stages* of language learning, the pedagogical factors which we have noted above still apply but, in addition, we can provide for written work on a more extensive scale and in particular integrate it more effectively with other skills (see Chapter 8). At this level, the written language itself will also provide contexts for learning — through reading — and writing activities may be related to these. At the same time, both here and at the post-intermediate level, writing may become *a goal in itself*. Although in language programmes which do not have a specific orientation we are not in a position to predict which students are likely to have a need for writing as one of the outcomes of their course, most students will have to do some form of written examination and this will increase their motivation to learn to write well. In addition, we can identify and concentrate on forms of writing which have a *practical* value, the relevance of which should be easily apparent to the learners. Specific needs can also be met because writing practice can to some extent be individualised.

Clearly, however, the situation is so complex that there is no one set of answers, although this applies to the teaching of other skills too. But on pedagogical grounds alone it would seem that writing is a skill worth developing in the foreign language. Our problem is how to do this in such a way that the learners see the *purpose* of writing and make measurable progress through the performance of realistic and relevant tasks.

**Discussion**

1 Which of the differences between speech and writing, listed in the table on page 3, do you think are especially important when teaching writing?
2 From your own experience of teaching (or learning) a foreign language, do you agree that writing is worth teaching on pedagogical grounds alone?

**Exercises**

1 It was said in 1.1 that we do not know much about individual methods of composing a text. Note down some of the things you do when you are writing and compare them with a friend.

*This term is used here and elsewhere to refer to language which is presented and practised orally (for example, through dialogues and related activities). It does not imply that the learners have not *seen* the written form.

2 *We produce a sequence of sentences . . . linked together in certain ways.* Reread 1.1 and make a list of some of the linking devices used.
3 Make a list of the things you use writing for. Arrange them as follows:

| | PERSONAL | PROFESSIONAL |
|---|---|---|
| Regular | | |
| Occasional | | |

Compare your list with a friend.
4 Write out a version of the conversation between the two speakers in 1.4.2 in normal written prose style.

**References***

1 The corrected draft on page 2 comes from J Barzun and HF Graff: *The Modern Researcher* (1970). The transcript of spoken English on page 4 comes from the *David Freeman Show* (1985), in which David Freeman interviews professional musicians.
2 On writing see J Britton in A Davies (1975): *Teaching Writing*; F Smith (1982), S Krashen (1984) pages 4–19 and V Zamel (1981 and 1983).
3 On paralinguistic features see D Abercrombie in J Laver and S Hutcheson (1972): *Paralanguage*.
4 On the ways in which languages organise thought patterns in different ways see R B Kaplan in K Croft (1980): *Cultural Thought Patterns in Inter-Cultural Education*.
5 On the pedagogical value of writing see C Bratt Paulston (1972) pages 33–6. For a more extreme view of the value of teaching writing see M Sharwood-Smith (1976) pages 17–19.

*All references are to books and articles listed in the Bibliography on page 153.

# 2

# Learning to use the resources of the written language

## 2.1 Understanding how the written language functions

One of our major tasks is to familiarise the learners with the devices that are needed for effective communication through the medium of writing. In extent, this is not unlike the task we have in teaching the appropriate use of stress and intonation for oral communication. In both cases an awareness of how language functions as a communication system can only be taught through adequate exposure to the language and through activities which lead to an understanding of the devices which the language employs. Of the two, exposure is the more important.

For this reason, reading will play an extremely important part in the development of writing ability because, although in itself it will not produce good writers, it appears to be an essential pre-condition. Reading may of course be a goal in its own right and in any case is likely to be a more important one than writing. But the two skills can and should be developed in close collaboration. In any case, true understanding of a text — any type of text ranging from an informal letter to the formal exposition of some highly factual topic — depends on an appreciation of the devices which the writer has employed in order to convey his meaning through the medium of writing. This appreciation is an important step towards effective writing.

To develop this understanding it is not enough to focus attention on those bits of information which the reader can easily retrieve from the text at a superficial level of understanding. This type of activity may be a useful expedient for certain kinds of oral practice, but it does not significantly help the learners to understand *how* the writer is getting his meaning across, and therefore, in the long run, does not contribute greatly to reading efficiency. We need to get them to examine the text at a much deeper level. In time it is hoped that they will begin to do this more or less intuitively.

Two examples of how texts can be dealt with for this purpose are given on the next page.

### 2.1.1 Personal communication

The first example we shall examine is a letter. The text is a piece of personal communication: the writer knows his reader and we may assume that he had reasons for *writing* to him, rather than *speaking* to him directly (for example, on the phone).

92 Mount Road
London
NW10 3YE
October 10 1987

Dear Mike,
Sorry I wasn't able to get to your party last Saturday. I was all ready to come and just about to leave when I got a phone call from a friend. He had just arrived from Teheran - on his way to Canada - and he wanted to spend the evening with me before he left the next morning. Well, I couldn't refuse, could I? Of course I tried to phone you, but your number was engaged. And after that I was busy with my friend all evening.
I hope you'll understand. I know you needed my records, but I'm sure you all had a marvellous time just the same. <u>My</u> evening, as it turned out, was rather boring.
Hope to see you soon.

Yours,
Nick

What, then, are the kinds of thing we can do in order to get the learners to look at this letter *as a piece of personal communication*? A possible approach is outlined here.

(a) *What is the writer's purpose?*

That is, we want the students to decide why Nick is writing to Mike. If they can recognise that Nick is apologising and giving his reasons (or excuses!) for not doing something, then they have identified the overall communicative purpose of the letter. In this case it is fairly obvious, but in other contexts it may be harder to elucidate. The point of the activity is to demonstrate that understanding the writer's communicative purpose is an essential part of understanding the text.

(b) *How does the writer achieve his purpose?*

Here we get the students to consider some of the ways in which the writer does this. For example, how does he apologise? How does he try to assure Mike that he intended to come to his party? How does he assure him that he tried to get in touch with him? What is the significance of: *Well, I couldn't refuse, could I?* and *I know you needed my records*? Why does he mention that he had such a boring evening himself? It is through questions of this kind that we can begin to get the students to understand why the writer wrote certain things and expressed them in a certain way.

(c) *How does the writer establish and maintain contact with his reader?*

Here we can get the students to look both at the language in general and at particular expressions to draw their attention to the ways in which he does this. In this letter it is done partly through the informal style, which reflects certain features of conversational English (for example, the use of contracted forms such as *wasn't, couldn't* and ellipsis: *Sorry I wasn't able*) and partly through appealing to his reader directly with: *Well, I couldn't refuse, could I?* and *I hope you'll understand*.

(d) *What typical features of written English are there in the text?*

Here we will get the students to look at features such as linking devices, sentence structure and inter-sentence structure. While we would not expect to find a great many samples within the context of an informal letter such as this (the third sentence provides the best example, with cohesion through the use of the pronoun *he* and the structure of the sentence itself), we want them to appreciate that *this is not speech written down*, however informal the style may be and however much it reflects certain features of conversational English. To reinforce this point, we might get them to transform the letter into a conversation, which, even though it is hypothetical, will underline the differences between the two mediums of communication. A conversation between Nick and Mike might have gone something like this:

NICK: Look, Mike, I'm terribly sorry I couldn't get to your party . . .
MIKE: Yeah . . . why didn't you phone?
NICK: Well, I did try . . . I just couldn't get through . . .
MIKE: So what happened, then?
NICK: Well, just at the last minute . . . I was just about to leave in fact . . . and the phone rang and, well, I've got this friend in Teheran, you see, and . . . (etc.)

Finally, we might get the students to compare this letter with a formal note of apology, such as this:

> I regret that I was unable to attend the party to which you so kindly invited me, due to circumstances beyond my control. Please accept my sincere apologies.

We might also ask them to consider the circumstances in which such a note might have been written and why, unlike Nick, the writer does not go into the reasons for his not going to the party.

### 2.1.2 Non-personal communication

For our second example, we shall look at a piece of expository writing.* Unlike the text in 2.1.1, it is not addressed to a person known to the writer.

> Electricity is the most useful form of energy there is. It is easy to produce; it can be transmitted over long distances; it is clean to use and it has no smell. Above all, it is convenient.
>
> The electricity produced by nature — lightning — is a different kind of electricity from that which flows through an electric light bulb. It is called static electricity, because it exerts a force which is stationary. It is easy to demonstrate electrostatic attraction. Rub a comb on the sleeve of your jersey. This will charge the comb with static electricity, and it will now pick up small pieces of paper.
>
> The other kind of electricity needs to flow in order to have any effect. The electricity in a battery, for example, will not make a light bulb glow until bulb and battery are linked by wires through which the electricity can flow. This kind of electricity is often called current electricity; the wire 'channel' through which it flows is known as the circuit.

This kind of text is clearly very different from the one in 2.1.1. As we have noted, the writer is not addressing anyone in particular, at least not anyone known to him personally. However, we must assume that he has *some sort of reader* in mind, and that this is relevant to the way he writes. We might begin, therefore, by trying to get the students to identify what sort of person this is. If we examine the text, we find that the writer is presenting some basic information on the subject of electricity. The reader he is addressing, then, whom he keeps in mind throughout, is presumably someone who knows little or nothing about the subject, and his purpose, his communicative goal, is to *inform* him of some basic facts.

Having established the writer's intention, we might then get the students to consider how he goes about *presenting* these basic facts to the reader. We could begin by inviting them to consider, in a general way, on the basis of their experience, what we normally do in a situation like this when we want to get

*From The Sampson Low Great World Encyclopaedia (1975).

across some information to a person who is unfamiliar with the subject. Some useful questions to ask the students would be:

— How important is it to *sequence* the various pieces of information? (What happens, for example, if the various pieces of information are jumbled up?)
— How does it help to *compare* and *contrast* certain items?
— What is the purpose of *giving examples*?
— How important is it to *define* new terms and how do we do it?

We can then move from the general experience of the students to an examination of the text itself. At this stage some useful questions to ask would be:

— How has the writer sequenced his information?
— Has he separated one piece of information from another? (How has he done it?)
— Has he made any comparisons or contrasts? (How do these help the reader to understand the subject matter?)
— Has he defined any terms? (How has he done it?)

Our examination of the text along these lines should help the students to see, in particular, that the structuring of the second and third paragraphs is quite deliberate: the writer *might* have gone about it in a different way but what he *chose* to do was to deal first with one type of electricity and then with another, contrasting the two kinds and supporting each with examples.

We can draw attention to the overall structure of the text through some sort of diagrammatic analysis. For example:

*Para 1*: Introductory statement about the value of electricity
Supporting statements as examples of its value

*Para 2*: First type of electricity contrasted with the second
Definition of term
Example

*Para 3*: Second type of electricity
Example
Definition of terms

Even a simple breakdown like this will help the students to appreciate not only that the text has an *identifiable structure* but also that it is this structure, together with the language through which it is realised, that enables the writer to communicate effectively with his reader.

Finally, we can get the students to look at some of the linguistic devices which the writer has used. Some of these serve to unify the text, while others realise the organisational structure outlined above. These devices are examined in greater detail in 2.2.2. Here, however, we might note the *variety* of ways in which the writer presents his *examples* to the reader.

*Para 1*: He uses a series of supporting statements.

*Para 2*: He makes a direct appeal to the reader to carry out a simple experiment.

*Para 3*: He provides a concrete example.

We should also note how he unifies his text through devices such as *The other kind of . . . This kind of . . .* and through the use of the pronoun form *it* alternated with repetition of the key lexical item *electricity*.

### 2.1.3 Pedagogical implications

We cannot pretend that analysis of texts along these lines will *by itself* enable the students to learn to write effectively. This can only be achieved through adequate exposure to the written language backed up by appropriate practice. But, given the problems of expressing oneself through the medium of writing, it would seem that some *explicit* examination of how we communicate through writing is an indispensable part of the programme. In particular, it serves to make the students aware that *any piece of writing is an attempt to communicate something: that the writer has a goal or purpose in mind; that he has to establish and maintain contact with his reader; that he has to organise his material and that he does this through the use of certain logical and grammatical devices.*

We shall of course have to examine a great many different kinds of writing and it is assumed that the analysis of texts along these lines would be an ongoing activity, carried out at different levels of difficulty at different stages of the programme. In the early stages we shall have to use the students' mother tongue for this purpose, otherwise they may miss the finer points of the analysis. Later on, we shall also want to refine our two types of writing and establish sub-types: different kinds of letters, reports, narrative texts and so on. But the basic distinction which has been drawn — between those situations in which the writer is addressing someone he knows and those in which he is writing in some kind of institutional capacity — is a fundamental one. Each type of writing has its own value, both in terms of developing writing skills and for the learners personally.

## 2.2 The resources of the written language

When we speak of the written language and its resources, this should not be taken to imply that we can draw any sharp dividing line between the language used in speech and the language used in writing. Rather, we have two independent but interrelated forms, embodied, at the level of phonology and graphology, in two different mediums. Both the spoken and the written forms *can* draw on the same linguistic resources of the language, its grammar and lexis, but the extent to which they draw on some resources rather than on others relates largely to the nature of the two channels: speech as the language of immediate communication; writing as the way of making contact at a distance.

Thus, certain types of sentence structure, such as non-restrictive clauses (for example: *This type of clause, which is rarely heard in speech, is quite common in writing*) are more typical of the written language, but they *may* occur in speech. However, to take the example of non-restrictive clauses, speech has its own way of handling parenthetic constructions. For example: *This type of clause — you don't often hear it in speech — is quite common in writing*.

Similarly, most sentence-linking devices and those used to express logical relationships also occur in the spoken language but, because of the *nature* of the channel (the immediacy of the listener, the possibility of interaction), they are less frequent than in writing, where they are essential for the construction of a text which has to be understood without further help from the writer.

In general, therefore, it can be said that our purpose in selecting certain types of sentence structure rather than others and in making greater use of linking and other devices is determined by the need to make the meaning of the text as *explicit* as possible. Thus in speech an utterance such as:

John *may* go.

is clear. In writing, however, we may have to use a different kind of modal construction which does not depend on intonation. For example:

There is a possibility that John will go.

Similarly, in speech:

*John* did it.

is clear, but in writing we can help our reader by using an alternative construction such as:

It was John who did it.

In the written form of the language, then, there is greater reliance on the structural elements alone and this, together with the time the writer has for organising his text, accounts for the higher frequency of certain structures.

### 2.2.1 Graphological resources

These include spelling, punctuation and other devices which the written language makes use of in order to convey patterns of meaning. This section is not intended to provide a spelling or punctuation guide but rather to assess the value of these features as part of the resources of the written form of the language and therefore their relative importance in a writing programme.

(a) *Spelling*

Mastery of the writing system *includes* the ability to spell. However, because in English the relationship between sound and symbol is a complex one,* spelling is a problem for many users of the language, native and non-native speakers alike, and most of us are obliged to consult a dictionary from time to time. While we do not want to encourage the learners to be indifferent towards spelling, we should acknowledge that mis-spelling rarely interferes with communication — in fact, English spelling was not standardised until the eighteenth century — any more than, on a phonemic level, mistakes of pronunciation greatly affect intelligibility.

It is inappropriate, therefore, in a writing programme, to adopt too prescriptive an attitude towards spelling. This tends to be encouraged by the fact that writing is open to inspection and is used in tests and examinations. Responsibility for ensuring an *adequate* mastery of spelling should be divided between the teacher and the learner: it is the teacher's responsibility to provide guidance in key areas, through rules, since English spelling is by no means unsystematic and much help can be given in

*There are forty-four phonemes in English and twenty-six letters of the alphabet. In the orthographic system, letters are combined to form different symbols (e.g. *n* and *ng*) while some symbols do double duty (e.g. *y* represents both the /j/ and /i/ phonemes).

this way, while it is the learner's task to consult a dictionary for guidance. This habit will be greatly encouraged by *drawing attention* to mistakes rather than *correcting* them (see Chapter 10). On the whole, however, spelling efficiency and improvement is likely to relate to reading (i.e. the amount of exposure) and this again emphasises the importance of reading in developing writing ability.

(b) *Punctuation*

Except in a few areas, the conventions governing the use of the visual devices known as punctuation are fairly well established, although punctuation has never been standardised to the same extent as spelling. Attitudes, therefore, tend to be fairly prescriptive, extending even into areas where variation in usage is tolerated. The result of this is that the learners are inclined to treat punctuation as something that can be done mechanically and as an 'extra' rather than as an essential part of the writing system.

The *communicative value* of punctuation needs to be *demonstrated*. For example, it is precisely because the reader expects sentence boundaries to be marked (with a capital letter at the start and a full stop, or some equivalent device, at the close) and because he expects questions to be signalled with a question mark, even though the presence of this symbol may be redundant in most cases, that these conventions cannot be ignored. Similarly, at a higher level, the reader expects to have paragraphs marked for him, normally by finding the opening sentence indented and the rest of the line after the last sentence left blank. These conventions tell him that the writer intends this set of sentences to be taken together. On the other hand, with devices such as commas and semi-colons, there is great variation both in how they are used and the extent to which they are used, and this should be freely acknowledged. We should also admit that there are areas of difficulty for most of us, such as the use of hyphens in compound nouns, where recourse to a dictionary is the only solution.

In the area of punctuation, then, we can best help the students if we provide them with guidance that is not too rigidly prescriptive, and at the same time encourage them to consider the effect on the reader if, for example, sentence and paragraph boundaries are *not* marked. Likewise, instead of criticising a sentence or a paragraph for being 'too long', we might ask them to consider whether it places a strain on the reader in any way. Some punctuation devices admittedly call for a cautious use (for example, the use of exclamation marks and dashes) and here there is no harm in telling our students to use them sparingly. On the other hand, it would be wrong to deny the learners an expedient such as underlining words or phrases that call for special emphasis, since this is the equivalent of italicisation in print.

(c) *Other graphological resources*

Other graphological resources which form part of the wide range of devices available to us in the writing system include the use of headings, footnotes, tables of contents and indexes. These will not be relevant to all our students, but at least they should be aware that a heading enables the writer to give his reader some advance notice of what to expect, while a footnote enables him to extract a supplementary piece of information from the text and still make it accessible to the reader.

### 2.2.2 Rhetorical resources

This term is used to refer to all the devices which are needed in writing in order to produce a text in which the sentences are organised into a coherent whole, in such a way that they fulfil the writer's communicative purpose. This section is intended to provide a brief survey of these resources. A more detailed list, together with examples, is given in the Appendix.

Rhetorical devices are looked at here under three headings: *logical, grammatical* and *lexical*.

(a) *Logical devices*

Logical devices are words or phrases which indicate meaning relationships between or within sentences. These include those of addition, comparison, contrast, result, exemplification and so on (some of these we have already looked at in 2.2.2). It is through devices such as these that the writer is able to organise his ideas and to help his reader follow him from one sentence to another.

To express *addition*, we may, for example, use the co-ordinator *and*, but other devices are available to us, such as *furthermore, moreover, besides, in addition (to . . .), what is more*, etc. The appropriate use of one of these devices tells the reader that two sentences are intended to be taken together. For example:

> The public library has 21,000 books which can be taken out on loan. In addition, there is a reference section of over 6,000 volumes.

Similarly with the relationship of *contrast*: this may be signalled through the co-ordinator *but* or by using *however, yet, while, on the other hand*, etc. For example (to continue the sequence above):

> . . . In addition there is a reference section of over 6,000 volumes. Many of the books in this section, *however*, are not kept on the shelves and are only available to the public on request.

Through the use of *however* the writer has signalled a difference between the part of the library which contains the books that can be borrowed (and are on the shelves) and the reference section, where some books are stored separately.

We have seen in 2.1.2 how important these devices are in presenting ideas so that the text has a clear structure. This helps the reader to follow the writer's thought. In certain types of text, it would be extremely difficult to organise the content effectively without the appropriate use of devices for *enumeration (first(ly), in the first place, second(ly) . . . finally, last of all,* etc.) and for *summarising (in short, on the whole,* etc.).

(b) *Grammatical devices*

Equally important for the cohesion of a text are the links established by certain grammatical devices, such as those, for example, which signal relationships between sentences by means of *back reference* (or *anaphora*). There are several instances of this type of linking in the text in 2.1.2. For example:

> *Electricity* is the most useful form of energy there is. It is easy to use; it can be transmitted over long distances (etc.).

Here the link between the sentences is established through the use of the pronominal form *it*. The examination of almost any text will reveal that this is an extremely common way of binding sentences together and giving a text cohesion. It is not a device, however, whose value is immediately appreciated by non-native users of the language.

Back reference binding two sentences together may also be effected by means of a *deictic*, such as a demonstrative adjective or pronoun or an article. For example, in (a) above we had:

> In addition, there is a reference section of over 6,000 volumes. Many of the books in this section, however, . . .

In the text in 2.1.2 we had:

> Rub a comb on the sleeve of your jersey. This will charge the comb with static electricity.

*This* links the second sentence with the whole of the preceding one. Compare, for example:

> Go to the reference section. This is where you will find the books you need.

Here the link through *this* is only with part of the preceding sentence: *the reference section*.

The text in 2.1.2 also provides an example of the anaphoric use of *the*.

> Rub a comb on the sleeve of your jersey. This will charge the comb with static electricity.

Here the use of *the* signals to the reader that the writer is referring to the comb mentioned in the previous sentence.

Finally, we should note that sentences are frequently linked through a change of word or phrase order: for example, by placing a word or phrase in the front position in the sentence:

> Go to the reference library. Here you will find the books you need.

> John worked in the library between 1970 and 1975. At that time, the library . . .

(c) *Lexical devices*

Almost any text displays a great deal of cohesion on a lexical level. To some extent this might be felt to be inevitable, but nevertheless this is another significant way in which sentences are linked together.

Key words, for example, are often repeated: *electricity* occurs ten times in the text in 2.1.2 although it is also replaced by *it* to give grammatical cohesion. Key items are also repeated in different forms: thus, in the text in 2.1.2 we have not only *electricity* but also *electric* and *electrostatic*. Another common device is the use of a synonymous word or phrase. For instance, in the first example in (a) above we have *books* in the first sentence and *volumes* in the second.

### 2.2.3 Pedagogical implications

The pedagogical problems we are faced with in this area are clearly considerable. For the most part, oral work will have focused mainly on a mastery of *sentence structure*, which in itself is a formidable learning task, with little or no attention being paid to the way in which sentences are linked or sequenced. In any case, as we have seen, the nature of the medium calls for a different kind of organisation, much more rigorous than in speech, so that, even if the learners are *familiar* with some of these devices, they will still have to learn how to use them in writing. The writing programme requires, therefore, both an *extensive understanding* of these resources and *considerable practice* in using them in appropriate forms of written expression.

Analysis of texts can contribute significantly to the learners' understanding of these devices. In particular, we might note that many students are simply not *aware*, for example, how the use of the pronominal forms and other substitution devices contribute to the cohesion of a text (in their mother tongue the subject pronominal forms such as *he, she, it, they* may even be *optional* elements in sentence structure). The use of adverbial words and phrases in the front position in the sentence (referred to on page 18) will probably require special teaching, since on the whole this will have been discouraged for *oral* production. In oral work, it is often a problem to get the learners to use: *There was a book on the table*, whereas: *On the table there was a book* might be the appropriate form in a written *sequence* of sentences.

The logical devices may also present problems on a conceptual level. The learners have to understand not only the semantic differences between one type of device and another, but also the different shades of meaning between one item and another, since they are not all freely interchangeable. There is obviously considerable danger, therefore, in exposing the students to too many of these devices at one time (for example, in the form of a list). Their introduction into the writing programme must be gradual and systematic. At the same time, however, since all the devices — logical, grammatical and lexical — occur simultaneously in a text and since sentences intended to be taken together commonly display more than one linking feature, it does not seem feasible or even desirable to try to deal with these different kinds of linking devices separately. This problem is looked at again in 3.3.

**Discussion**

1 Do you agree that reading is an important factor in teaching writing?
2 Why is it important to try to get students to understand a writer's communicative purpose?
3 Do you agree that it is necessary to pay attention to spelling and punctuation?
4 From your experience of teaching (or learning) a foreign language, do you think that the rhetorical devices listed in 2.2.2 could be picked up (e.g. from reading) or need to be taught systematically?

**Exercises**

1 Repeat Exercise 2 on page 8, which you first attempted after reading Chapter 1.
2 In 2.1.1 (d) you have the beginning of a conversation between Nick and Mike. Suggest how it might continue.
3 Read the following text carefully:

Smoking, which may be a pleasure for some people, is a source of serious discomfort for their fellows. Further, medical authorities express their concern about the effect of smoking on the health not only of those who smoke but also those who must involuntarily inhale the contribution of the smokers to the atmosphere.

As you are doubtless aware, a considerable number of our students have joined together in an effort to persuade the university to ban smoking in the classrooms. I believe they are entirely right in their aim. However, I would hope that it is possible to achieve this by an appeal to reason and to concern for others rather than by regulation.

Smoking is prohibited by City by-laws in theatres and in halls used for showing films as well as laboratories where there may be a fire hazard. Elsewhere, it is up to your own good sense.

I am therefore asking you to maintain 'No Smoking' in the auditoria, classrooms and seminar rooms where you teach. This proof of your interest for their health and well-being is very important to a large number of our students.

In the first paragraph, back reference has been indicated by means of a circle and an arrow. Other linking devices have been boxed. Mark the rest of the text in the same way.

**References**

1 On the importance of teaching comprehension of a text, see A Davies and H G Widdowson in J P B Allen and S Pit Corder (1974) *Reading and Writing*.
2 On spelling, see J Pearce in P Doughty, J Pearce and G Thornton (1972) *Spoken and Written*. For spelling rules, see R A Close (1975) and E Abbott (1979).
3 On punctuation, see R Quirk et al (1972) and R A Close (1975).
4 On the rhetorical resources of the written language, see A Tadros in D L Bouchard and L J Spaventa (1980) and V Horn (1972). The division into logical, grammatical and lexical is based on the description given by Tadros. For more extensive treatments of cohesion, see R Quirk (1972) *Sentence Connection* and M A K Halliday and R Hasan (1976).

# 3

# General principles for teaching writing

## 3.1 Approaches to teaching writing

Attempts to teach writing — since the time when students were merely given a topic of some kind and asked to produce a 'composition' without further help — have usually focused on some particular problematical aspect of the writing situation. Some key approaches are examined below.

### 3.1.1 Focus on accuracy

Mistakes show up in written work (especially since this is usually subject to rigorous 'correction') and not unnaturally come to be regarded as a major problem. It was assumed that students made mistakes because they were allowed to write what *they* wanted, and accuracy-oriented approaches have therefore stressed the importance of *control* in order to eliminate them from written work. Students are taught how to write and combine various sentence types and manipulation exercises like the one below are used to give them the experience of writing connected sentences.

> A (1) man (2) walked (3) down the street. A (4) girl (5) was waiting for him outside a (6) shop. As he approached, she smiled (7) and said, 'Hello. How are you?'
>
> (1) tall, young, well-dressed
> (2) with a beard, in a black hat, with sunglasses
> (3) rapidly, hurriedly, impatiently
> (4) pretty, fair-haired, dark-skinned
> (5) in high-heeled shoes, with an umbrella, in a pink hat
> (6) chemist's, grocer's, bicycle
> (7) pleasantly, attractively, in a friendly manner

Gradually the amount of control is reduced and the students are asked to exercise meaningful choice (in the example above they do not have to think and they cannot make mistakes). At a still later stage, they may be given a good deal of guidance with language and content, but allowed some opportunities for self-expression.

This controlled-to-free approach was very much a product of the audio-lingual period, with its emphasis on step-by-step learning and formal correctness. Many such schemes were carefully thought out and, although no longer fashionable, they produced many useful ideas on how to guide writing.

### 3.1.2 Focus on fluency

In contrast, this approach encourages students to write as much as possible and as quickly as possible — without worrying about making mistakes. The important thing is to get one's ideas down on paper. In this way students feel that they are actually *writing*, not merely doing 'exercises' of some kind; they write what *they* want to write and consequently writing is an enjoyable experience.

Although this approach does not solve some of the problems which students have when they come to write in a foreign language (see 4.1), it draws attention to certain points we need to keep in mind. Many students write badly because they do not write *enough* and for the same reason they feel inhibited when they pick up a pen. Most of us write less well if we are *obliged* to write about something. A fluency-approach, perhaps channelled into something like keeping a diary, can be a useful antidote.

### 3.1.3 Focus on text

This approach stresses the importance of the paragraph as the basic unit of written expression and is therefore mainly concerned to teach students how to construct and organise paragraphs. It uses a variety of techniques, singly and in combination, such as:

— forming paragraphs from jumbled sentences;

— writing parallel paragraphs;

— developing paragraphs from topic sentences (with or without cues).

Once again this approach identifies and tries to overcome one of the central problems in writing: getting students to express themselves effectively at a level beyond the sentence.

### 3.1.4 Focus on purpose

In real life, as we have seen, we normally have a *reason* for writing and we write to or for *somebody*. These are factors which have often been neglected in teaching and practising writing. Yet it is easy to devise situations which allow students to write purposefully: for example, they can write to one another in the classroom or use writing in roleplay situations.

Although, like fluency writing, this approach does not solve specific problems which students have when handling the written language, it does motivate them to write and shows how writing is a form of communication.

## 3.2 The state of the art

Although some writing schemes and programmes have tended to rely largely or exclusively on one or other of these approaches, in practice most teachers and textbook writers have drawn on more than one and have combined and modified them to suit their purpose.

In recent years classroom methodology has been heavily influenced by the communicative approach, with its emphasis on task-oriented activities that involve, where possible, the exchange of information and the free use of language, without undue concern for mistakes. Receptive skills are also given more prominence and students are exposed to a wide range of spoken and written language. A good deal of recommended writing practice directly reflects the main concerns of this approach, although in practice both teachers and textbook writers deal with the classroom situation pragmatically and therefore retain a good deal of controlled practice. In general, however, attention is paid to motivation and there is usually some room for self-expression, even at the lower levels, as the examples on page 24 show.

No less interesting and significant are some of the 'side effects' of the communicative approach. For example:

- Students get more opportunities to read (and also to read more interesting and naturally written texts) and this kind of exposure to the written language is beneficial to writing.
- Both listening and reading material have related activities (see 6.3.1), many of which lead to incidental writing of a natural kind, such as note-taking. This in turn can lead on to further writing, such as using the notes to write a report. The factual nature of much reading and listening material is also useful for related writing activities.
- Learners are encouraged to interact and the activities required for this often involve writing (e.g. questionnaires, quizzes, etc.). Many of these activities involve an element of 'fun', so that students often enjoy writing (without perhaps realising it).
- Students are encouraged to work together in pairs and groups and to share writing tasks. This removes the feeling of isolation which bothers many learners.

In spite of these advances, however, writing skills are still relatively neglected in many courses. Objectives are rarely spelt out as clearly as they are for oral work and there is an overall lack of guidance for the systematic development of written ability. It is likely, therefore, that many teachers will need to look for ways of supplementing their coursebooks if they want their students to become proficient in writing. This, in any case, will always be necessary, as with oral work, when trying to meet the individual needs of certain groups of students.

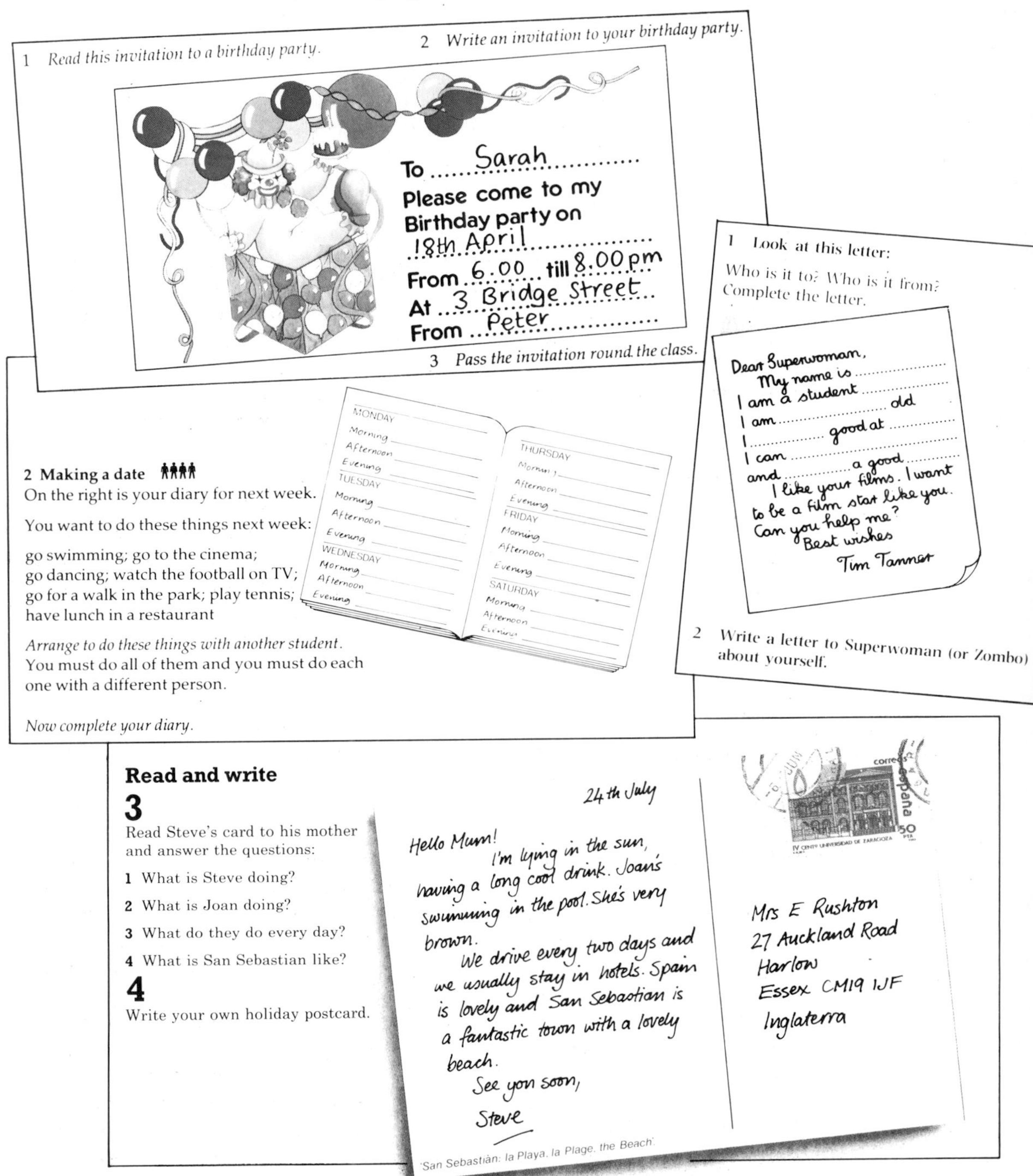

## 3.3 The role of guidance

In view of the many difficulties with which the students are faced in learning how to write a foreign language, the fundamental principle of *guiding* them in various ways towards a mastery of writing skills, and sometimes *controlling* what they write, is not one we can lightly dismiss, even if the principle has to some extent been misapplied (for example, in trying to eliminate mistakes). Rather, we should consider more carefully what kind of guidance we should give them, particularly in relation to the various problems they have when writing (see 1.4).

On a linguistic level, since our aim is to develop their ability to *write a text*, one way of helping the students, and therefore of providing guidance, is by *using the text as our basic format for practice*, even in the early stages. While this does not rule out some sort of sentence practice, which may be necessary for the mastery of certain types of compound and complex sentence structure, best practised *through* writing because they are most commonly used *in* writing (see 4.4), we do not need to build into the writing programme a step-by-step approach which will take the learners in easy stages from *sentence practice* to the production of a text. With the text as our basic format for practice, we can teach within its framework all the rhetorical devices — logical, grammatical and lexical — which the learners need to master. While we must be careful not to overwhelm them with too many difficulties at any one time (see 2.2.3), there is no apparent justification for attempting to separate features of the written language which go naturally together.

By using texts (letters and reports, for example — even dialogues in the early stages) as our basic practice format, rather than some other unit such as the sentence or even the paragraph, we can make writing activities much more meaningful for the students and thereby increase their motivation to write well. The text provides *a setting within which they can practise*, for example, sentence completion, sentence combination, paragraph construction, etc. in relation to longer stretches of discourse. In this way they can see not only *why* they are writing but also write in a manner *appropriate to the communicative goal of the text*.

This, then, is one way of helping the learners: by making writing tasks more realistic, by relating practice to a specific purpose instead of asking them to write simply for the sake of writing. In order to find our contexts for written work, we shall also need to explore opportunities for integrating it effectively with other classroom activities involving not only reading but also speaking and listening. Writing tends to get relegated to the level of exercises partly because it is treated as a compendium to the lesson rather than as a worthwhile learning activity in itself. While it is convenient, as we have acknowledged (see 1.6 (d)), to be able to set written work as homework and while writing may not come very high on the list of priorities, this does not mean that it cannot take its place as part of a natural sequence of learning activities.

A writing activity, for example, can derive in a natural way from some prior activity such as a conversation or something read. As in *real life*, it can be the consequence of a certain situation. We see an advertisement for a job, for example, which involves *reading*. We talk about it and perhaps phone up about it, which involves *speaking* and *listening*. We then decide to apply for the job — which involves *writing*. Although, perhaps, we cannot completely integrate writing with other activities without a radical change in materials design (see

8.3), there is much we can do to relate it more effectively to other classroom activities: for example, by extending the contexts which we have set up for oral work, through simple role-play activities, to provide a meaningful setting for writing activities as well. In this way we can hope to overcome some of the difficulties which the learners have with role projection for writing tasks.

So far we have looked at guidance in terms of what kind of framework — linguistic and contextual — we can provide in order to make writing tasks more purposeful rather than in terms of the actual support we can give the students in order to ensure that they complete their tasks with reasonable success. Since the major part of this book is concerned with an exploration of the various techniques and procedures we can use, at this stage we shall only stress that we need *a whole range of techniques*, each appropriate to specific goals and needs. Variety is important, as in oral work. This is essential for the sake of interest: the learners get bored if they are constantly asked to perform the same type of task. But another significant factor is that certain techniques are effective for developing particular writing skills. For example, texts (read or heard) provide the right sort of context for note-taking: they not only lead on to meaningful writing tasks but also provide a model for the kind of writing expected. Visual material, on the other hand, properly used (see Chapter 7) provides a more open-ended framework for writing activities of different kinds at different levels, but it is less suited for elementary writing activities than is often assumed. Particular kinds of visual material, such as diagrams and tables, are valuable for developing organisational skills. Clearly, then, our approach should be as eclectic as possible, using those forms of guidance which are appropriate to different kinds of writing at different levels of attainment.

One thing that needs special emphasis, however, is that guidance need not — indeed should not — imply tight control over what the learners write. If, for example, we accept that errors in speech are not only inevitable but are also a natural part of learning a language, then we should accept that they will occur, and to some extent should be allowed to occur, in writing too. Unless the learners are given opportunities to write what *they* want to write, they will never learn this skill. As in speech, when we provide opportunities for free expression, errors will occur, but this is a situation which we must accept. Perhaps it is largely our *attitude* towards these errors that is wrong: because they occur in writing, we feel that they must be corrected, whereas in speech, perhaps because it is more transient, we are inclined to be more tolerant.

This is far from suggesting that free expression is the solution to learning to write: on the contrary, the learners have need of guidance, as they do with oral work. They must also be encouraged to look critically at what they write and taught to draft, correct and rewrite. But since no approach to teaching writing has yet been devised which will take them smoothly from writing under control to free expression, it seems reasonable to provide some opportunities for writing freely, even in the early stages, as we do for oral work. This will not only enable us to see whether the students are making any real progress; it will also ensure that they become *learners* rather than *leaners*.

## 3.4 The needs of the learners

In this section some of the main issues of Chapters 1-3 are reviewed. They are now presented in the form of guidelines for a writing programme.

(a) *Teach the learners how to write.*

The ability to write is all too often assumed, especially if the learners are mature, can write reasonably well in their mother tongue and have also acquired some proficiency in the spoken language. But oral skills — both listening and speaking — have to be taught, through appropriate techniques and through appropriate forms of practice. Since the spoken and written forms of the language are not the same and since writing is a different way of communicating from speech, it follows that *writing skills require special teaching* too.

(b) *Provide adequate and relevant experience of the written language.*

We work on the principle that oral ability requires a firm foundation in *listening* and that the latter must be on a broader basis than speaking. Similarly, writing has to be preceded and accompanied by wide exposure to appropriate models of written language. If the learners have only seen dialogues in their textbooks and narrative prose in their readers, they cannot be expected to produce other varieties of the written language appropriate, for example, to letters or reports.

(c) *Show the learners how the written language functions as a system of communication.*

*Exposure* to the written form of the language by itself is not sufficient. The learners also have to be made aware of how we communicate through the written medium and how this differs from speech. In particular, they need to be shown that any piece of writing, whether or not it is addressed to a specific reader, has a communicative purpose. They need to understand, therefore, how the resources of the written language are used to fulfil this purpose, by establishing and maintaining contact with the reader in order to get one's 'message' across.

(d) *Teach the learners how to write texts.*

We have already seen that writing, at least in any significant form, involves the ability to organise sentences into a coherent whole or text. Most writing practice should from the start aim to teach those devices of the written language (as identified in 2.2.2) which are needed to write various types of text. The practice of these devices should, wherever possible, be within the framework of a text which has a definite communicative goal, so that the learners see the *purpose* of what they are writing. The learners must also be given opportunities to practise organising their ideas to form acceptable paragraphs.

(e) *Teach the learners how to write different kinds of texts.*

The learners cannot be expected to master all the different varieties of the written form of the language. Many of them, in any case, would not be relevant to their needs, to the extent that these can be identified in a writing programme. At the same time, it is not enough to try to teach them a kind of 'neutral' general purpose form of written expression. As in speech, they have to some extent at least to be able to select an appropriate style, formal or informal, depending on what they are writing about and whom they are addressing, and to be able to present this to the reader in an appropriate form, such as a letter or a report. Although it cannot be said that this is easy, many of the difficulties which the learners have in this area arise because of the nature of the writing tasks: for example, simply being asked to write a paragraph out of context. Also, this kind of task does not encourage them to think of writing as communication. Likewise, it might be noted, our goal should not be to teach different kinds of writing (such as narrative, descriptive, expository and so on) but rather to see that these are practised within the wider context of a text. For example, a letter may involve some 'narration' (see the letter in 2.1.1) or 'description', while a report might provide the setting for some expository writing.

(f) *Make writing tasks realistic and relevant.*

All too often writing tasks *lack reality* for the learners because they do not give them the feeling that they are writing *to* or *for* somebody. They are done solely as a form of exercise for the benefit of the teacher, who reacts to them more like a judge than a genuine reader! The use of texts as the basic format for practice (see (d)) is only part of the solution. We must also attempt to identify those forms of writing which are most likely to be relevant to the learners' needs, such as various types of personal communication (notes, letters) and 'institutional' communication (formal letters, reports) and to establish classroom contexts for practising them (as suggested in 3.3. This aspect is further developed in 4.5 and 5.5). This does not rule out the possibility of other kinds of writing (for example, creative writing, such as stories, although of course at a fairly low level), provided the motivation for this kind of work can be established.

(g) *Integrate writing with other skills.*

Writing tends to be the 'Cinderella' of the four skills (at least at the lower levels) and is often relegated to the end of the teaching unit and used mainly for homework. This is unlikely to make the learners *want* to write. Where possible, we should introduce writing activities that lead naturally onto or from the use of other skills, so that the learners see writing as a *real* activity.

(h) *Use a variety of techniques and practice formats.*

This is important because the learners get bored with the same type of activity (however worthy!). Also, as we have seen, some techniques and formats are appropriate to certain levels. For example, letter writing is especially suitable for use in the early stages because it permits the learners to make some use of the spoken forms of the language within a new framework. We must also recognise that, in terms of developing writing skills, we cannot be sure how effective any single technique is.

(i) *Provide appropriate support.*

We have already noted (in 3.3) the importance of guidance and how, broadly, it can be interpreted in the writing programme in a variety of ways. It has been argued that guidance should be tempered with opportunities for free expression. We should remember, however, that writing tasks are generally *imposed* and that the learners may not have either the relevant ideas, when this involves some contribution on their part, or be sufficiently stimulated by the tasks to think of them. The problem is further compounded by their having to work on their own. Clearly there are many solutions to this problem and they need to be explored in a flexible way. In particular, however, the use of techniques and procedures which have proved valuable for oral work, such as pair and group work, need to be examined within the context of the writing programme. There seems no reason why, in the classroom at least, writing need be a solitary activity.

(j) *Be sympathetic!*

We have considered at length the many problems involved in writing and these are freely acknowledged to prevail when we write in our mother tongue, not only in a foreign language. Except in specialised programmes, heavily weighted in favour of reading and writing skills, we cannot expect too high a level of proficiency. With the help of a programme which takes the learners' problems into account, we can hope to make writing a more rewarding activity for them, both in terms of attainment and satisfaction. But we need to surrender our role as 'judges', except when writing is being tested or examined, and view what the learners write as attempts, however inadequate, to communicate. There is always a great temptation, perhaps a natural inclination, to concentrate on what is *wrong* in a piece of writing, mainly because, as we have already noted, it is there for us to read and reread. But if we are to be truly readers rather than judges, we should perhaps look not so much at what the learners have *failed* to achieve but rather at what they have actually *succeeded in doing*.

**Discussion**

1 Which of the approaches described in 3.1 do you think is most important? Why?
2 What reasons are given for taking the text as the basic format for practice? Do you agree with this proposal?
3 From your own experience of teaching (or learning) the written form of a foreign language, do you agree that free expression, as well as writing under control, should be a feature of the writing programme, even in the early stages?
4 In the guidelines for a writing programme in 3.4 why are the following points emphasised?
   (a) The learners have to be exposed to different varieties of the written form of the language.
   (b) The learners have to be set realistic tasks.
   (c) The learners' efforts need to be viewed sympathetically.
   Do you agree with these viewpoints?

**Exercises**

1 Examine any textbook of your own choosing to see what kinds of guided writing exercises are provided. In particular, consider whether the textbook writer tends to rely on a limited range of exercise types and whether he gives the learners any opportunities for free expression.
2 Rewrite the exercise in 3.1.1 so that a meaningful choice has to be made from the items provided.

**References**

1 For surveys of teaching writing, and in particular the use of guided writing, see C Bratt Paulston (1972). Also A Raimes and M Sharwood Smith in D L Bouchard and L J Spaventa (1980) and W Slager in *The Art of TESOL* (1982). Other accounts of teaching writing may be found in G Broughton et al (1978) and A Raimes (1983). For a description of the 'fluency' approach see Briere (1966).
2 The controlled writing exercise on page 22 comes from DH Spencer *Guided Composition Exercises* (Longman 1967). Not all the exercises in this book are manipulative.
3 For the purpose of writing this chapter, the following courses were surveyed for writing activities: B Abbs and I Freebairn *Strategies* (various levels) (Longman); S Axbey *Journeys* (Longman); J Blundell *Visa* (OUP); D Bolton and L Peterson *Breakaway* (Nelson); J Carmichael *Way Ahead* (Penguin); M Ellis and P Ellis *Counterpoint* (Nelson); J Harmer *Meridian* (Longman); B Hartley and P Viney *Streamline English* (OUP); R O'Neill *Kernel* (Longman); M Palmer and D Byrne *Track* (Longman); M Swan and C Walters *The Cambridge English Course* (CUP); M Vincent et al *Time for English* (Collins) and N Whitney *Checkpoint English* (OUP).
4 The illustrative material on page 24 comes from M Vincent et al *Time for English* (Collins ELT 1984) top; M Palmer and D Byrne *Track* (Longman 1982) centre left; J Carmichael *Way Ahead* (Penguin 1985) centre right, and J Harmer *Meridian* (Longman 1985) bottom.

# 4

# Writing in the early stages

## 4.1 Some basic considerations

In the early stages of a language course,* the principal factor which affects both the quantity and the kind of writing that can be done is the small amount of language that the learners have at their disposal — language which to a large extent they have acquired *orally* and to a lesser degree through reading.

The weighting, in favour of dialogue or narrative/descriptive type texts, may vary from one coursebook to another, but by and large we may assume that at this level patterns typical of the spoken language have been selected and that these are presented in contexts designed to promote oral fluency. We should also remember that the actual input of language is likely to be fairly slow: the students are learning how to understand and how to make themselves understood through the spoken medium. This is a situation which we have already contrasted with the one in the mother tongue classroom, when the learners first go to school (see 1.5).

One solution to this problem would be to delay the introduction of writing, at least in any significant form, until the learners have a much greater command of the language, in the form of a plateau on which written work could be much more easily based. However, if we adopted this solution, we should fail to satisfy needs which the learners have in the early stages and which can be met through writing: reinforcement of material learned orally, variety of activity in the classroom and increased contact with the language through work that can be done out of class (see 1.6). These are good reasons for introducing writing and it would be wrong to ignore them. In any case, although we have to work mainly within the limits of language which has been learned for oral purposes, it is possible to introduce a small number of items needed specifically for

*The first 75–90 hours or approximately the first year of a secondary school course. In some countries it is common for schoolchildren to have had some previous instruction in the language (e.g. at a middle school level) where the focus has been mainly on oral skills.

written work. These will enable us to make writing activities more interesting and also pave the way for more effective writing practice at a later stage.

### 4.1.1 The main features of the writing programme

Although most writing at this stage will be under control, we can and should avoid manipulative procedures which do not encourage the learners to think about what they write and which in any case do not help them to understand how the written language functions. We must also introduce activities which, however simple, demonstrate that writing can be used for the purpose of communication. Our objectives at this stage, however, must necessarily be modest.

The following goals are suggested:

(a) *Writing activities should satisfy immediate needs by providing the learners with opportunities for handling, through the medium of writing, language which they have learned orally.*

For this purpose, it is suggested that we should use dialogue writing as the *main* type of activity. This is a type of text which the students are familiar with; it provides a context for reinforcing and practising sentence structure and to some extent allows them to be creative.

(b) *Writing activities should also be forward-looking by beginning to familiarise the learners with patterns of language typical of the written medium: in particular, some of the devices needed for linking and sequencing sentences.*

For this purpose, *letter-writing* offers a format which has many advantages. If the letters are informal, the language used can to a large extent be based on what the learners have already learned orally, but at the same time we can introduce a small number of linking and sequencing devices (see 4.4). For the most part, then, 'exercises' to practise these devices will be embedded within the contexts of letters. An important point to note is that the students will also be *learning something new through writing*: for example, the layout of a letter, modes of address and certain opening and closing formulas.

(c) *Writing activities should also give the learners opportunities to communicate through writing and, equally important, simply to enjoy writing.*

Although we cannot afford to neglect other types of writing activity in the classroom situation, in the end for many students enjoyment may prove to be the most motivating factor.

You will need to get the right *balance* between these various types of activity so as to meet the needs of your particular students.

### 4.1.2 The role of the teacher

After selecting the appropriate writing activity (see 4.3 for examples):

(a) *Decide how to present the activity to the class.*

For example, in the early stages, it will help to do a certain amount of writing *with* the students, on the board or overhead projector. This is especially useful for the type of activity described in 4.4, where the students are learning something new, such as the use of certain connectives or the layout of a letter (etc). In particular, it also provides an opportunity to discuss alternative answers, reasons for certain choices and so on. On a simple level we can thus begin to demonstrate that writing is a thinking process.

(b) *Prepare the students orally.*

This should be regarded as a standard procedure for writing activities in the early stages (and later when introducing any new type of activity). Make sure, through a number of worked examples, that the students know exactly what they have to do. Do not, however, go through the whole task orally because this will leave the activity without any element of challenge and reduce interest in the actual writing task.

(c) *Decide how the writing task should be carried out.*

An activity may be done individually, in pairs or in small groups. Collaboration on a task, for example, will help to reduce the feeling of isolation which we noted in 1.4.1. Students also tend to get more involved in an activity if they are allowed to talk about it together rather than sit in silence. Some activities may be begun in pairs or in groups but concluded on an individual basis. In the early stages it would seem appropriate to allow many of the tasks to be done collaboratively except when feedback on individual progress is needed.

(d) *Decide on correction procedures.*

It is not essential or even desirable to examine everything the students write, although many students will want to have their work looked at. However, they can be asked to exchange their completed work and to evaluate one another's efforts. This helps to train them to look at written work critically, as *readers*, and will help them to view their own work in the same way at a later stage in the course. Work can also of course be discussed on a class basis and the students asked to make their own corrections.

### 4.1.3 The organisation of written work

In the course of the writing programme we shall be asking the students to carry out various kinds of activities. Some of these will of course have more permanent value than others, providing, for example, an index of the learners' progress in this skill, while other things they write may be needed for reference purposes (see, for example, 4.2.1). The question, therefore, of how they arrange their written work in their books is an important one. In any case, if the students are allowed to be casual, imposing no sort of organisation on their written work, writing is bound to seem less purposeful.

Ideally, perhaps, written work should be done on loose leaf sheets and arranged on a file, which has been divided into appropriate sections. Alternatively, one or more exercise books may be used for this purpose. For example, one book or one section of a book might consist of reference material which can be used for oral activities; another might contain work which has been done to develop a mastery of sentence structure, sentence combination and sentence sequencing; while a third one might be reserved for pieces of writing which demonstrate the communicative value of writing (for example, copies of the activities suggested in 4.5). In this way, all the material which the students produce is accessible both for future use or reference.

## 4.2 Copying as a writing activity

Some discussion of the value of copying is necessary because it is sometimes presented as the first stage in a writing programme. This of course will be the case if the learners have problems at the graphological level (that is, if they have to learn new graphic symbols or how to write from left to right). This aspect is dealt with in Chapter 12.

Equally commonly, however, copying is held to be valuable because it helps to teach spelling or to reinforce sentence structure. For example, we sometimes write words and sentences on the board and ask our students to copy them down. At the beginning of the course, such an activity may have a certain novelty value, and can of course serve to introduce the learners to the written form of what has been learned orally. But the novelty will soon wear off and copying will then become just one more classroom routine. Besides, what the learners copy tends to get lost in a jumble of notes made in the same way. One may well wonder whether this activity — like reading aloud — is not often just a way of filling in a little time in the lesson.

Yet copying need not be a pointless activity. Most of us would agree, on the basis of our own experience of trying to learn something new, that copying is an aid to retention. Furthermore, in real life, we frequently copy things down in order to have a *record* of them: for example, we copy addresses, the times of trains, telephone numbers as well as other bits of useful information or material for which we think we may have a future use. For example, we quite often make copies of songs and poems. The students can be asked to make their own copies of this type of material in a special notebook.

Copying, then, *can* be presented to the learners as a meaningful activity, particularly if we can get them to see it as a way of making a record of something which is not otherwise available to them (i.e. it does not appear in the textbook) or is not available to them in the *form* in which they have copied it (i.e. they have brought together certain data which is distributed in various lessons in their textbook). We must also demonstrate to them, through some activity either at the time or later, that they have done the copying to some purpose.

### 4.2.1 An example of meaningful copying

Vocabulary is an area which gives the students various kinds of learning problems, including spelling. It is also an area where it can be useful for them to have reference lists, in the form of lexical sets, such as clothes, furniture, food, etc. Let us take one such set — furniture — and see how we can present the compilation of a list of items as a purposeful copying task. The following steps are suggested.

(a) Ask the students to draw a plan of a house which includes the following rooms: kitchen, sitting-room, dining-room, bedroom and bathroom. Ask them to write in the names of the rooms on their plan.

(b) Ask them to dictate to you a list of items — furniture and some smaller objects (such as lamps, telephone, vase of flowers, etc.) — which could be found in any of these rooms. Write these on the board, asking the students to tell you how to spell them.

(c) Ask the students to use the list on the board to compile five lists, one for each room of their house, on a rough piece of paper. Each list should contain items which might be found in that room. An item may of course appear in more than one list (e.g. chair).

(d) Ask the students to put the items in each list in alphabetical order and to copy these lists into their exercise books. Each list should appear under its appropriate heading (e.g. kitchen, sitting-room, etc.).

(e) Ask the students to compare their lists with those of other students in the class.

Thus, what the students have compiled in their exercise books is a small reference section on furniture, which they should be encouraged to keep up to date by adding new items as they learn them. Although the activity was primarily a copying one — we may of course also allow them to include items which were not on the board — it also involved *thinking*: they had to divide up the list on the board, decide which items to include more than once and also to put them into alphabetical order.

Now that the students have made their reference list, which might be only one of many topic areas dealt with in the same or in a similar way, they should also be given an opportunity to *use* it: either in a writing activity, perhaps at some later stage, or in an oral activity for which reference to such a list might be called for. For example, lists of this kind are useful for certain types of language game which involve vocabulary repetition (such as variations on: *I went to the market and I bought . . .*).

### 4.2.2 Other copying activities

Notice that some of the activities in 4.2.1 mainly involve copying (e.g. (a)-(c)) since the students do not actually have to *contribute* to the text.

(a) *Putting a list of words in alphabetical order*

(b) *Putting a list of words in their correct sequence*

For example, days of the week, months, numbers.

(c) *Putting words in categories*

For example, arranging a list of words under headings:

| FOOD | ANIMALS | CLOTHES |
|---|---|---|
| | | |

(d) *Doing puzzles*

For example, here are the names of 11 countries:

Brazil, Egypt, England, France, Greece, India, Italy, Peru, Portugal, Spain, Turkey.

Complete the crossword. Which countries are not there?

(e) *Playing Bingo*

This involves selective copying and is an excellent way of revising vocabulary sets (e.g. colours, occupations, clothes, etc.) through a game.

A's list

| | |
|---|---|
| jacket | |
| socks | |
| jeans | |
| sweater | |
| shoes | |
| overcoat | |

B's list

| | |
|---|---|
| shirt | |
| overcoat | |
| gloves | |
| pullover | |
| hat | |
| socks | |

Write, with the help of suggestions from the class, 12–16 items on the board (e.g. for clothes: *jacket, hat, shirt, socks*, etc.). Ask the students to copy *any* words from the list. Then read out the words from the list *in any order*. The first student to hear all his words read out calls out BINGO!

From these suggestions it should be clear that copying need never be a boring activity! Some of the following activities, particularly dialogue writing, also involve copying; the students do not actually have to contribute to the text.

## 4.3 Reinforcement activities

Various ways of reinforcing language learned orally in the early stages are suggested below:*

### 4.3.1 Dialogue writing

(a) *Writing parallel dialogues with the help of keywords*

*Read this dialogue*:

A: Give me that book, please.
B: Which one?
A: The big one — on the table.
B: Here you are!
A: Thanks very much.

*Now use these keywords to write similar dialogues*:

(a) umbrella/red/behind/armchair
(b) box/small/on top of/cupboard
(c) hammer/heavy/near/window, etc.

(b) *Completing a dialogue, choosing from a list of jumbled sentences*

*Use these sentences, which are not in the correct order, to complete the dialogue below:*

I've never seen you there
I usually take my car
Mine's Jennie
At Clarkson's
Do you like it?

A: My name's Bob.
B: ...................

*These and all other examples in the book are intended to illustrate *types of activity*. The actual language used in the examples does not relate to any particular course.

A: Where do you work?
B: ....................
A: Really? I work there too.
B: ....................
A: Well, it's a big place and I only started last week.
B: ....................
A: It's not bad. Besides, I can now go to work by bus.
B: ....................
A: Do you? Well, perhaps you can give me a lift!

The students may also be asked to write a continuation of the dialogue.

(c) *Putting sentences in order to form a dialogue*

Instead of providing a dialogue frame, as in (b), all the sentences are jumbled up. It helps to number the first item, however, and also to limit the number of items to (say) eight.

(d) *Provide the students with a dialogue frame, similar to (b), which they have to complete with ideas of their own.*

4.3.2
Parallel writing

For this type of activity the students are given a model text of some kind and are asked to write a similar text with the help of cues. These may be verbal as in the first example below or visual as in the second. The text may recycle items of spoken or written language and can be used as an introduction to organising ideas in the form of a paragraph.

(a)

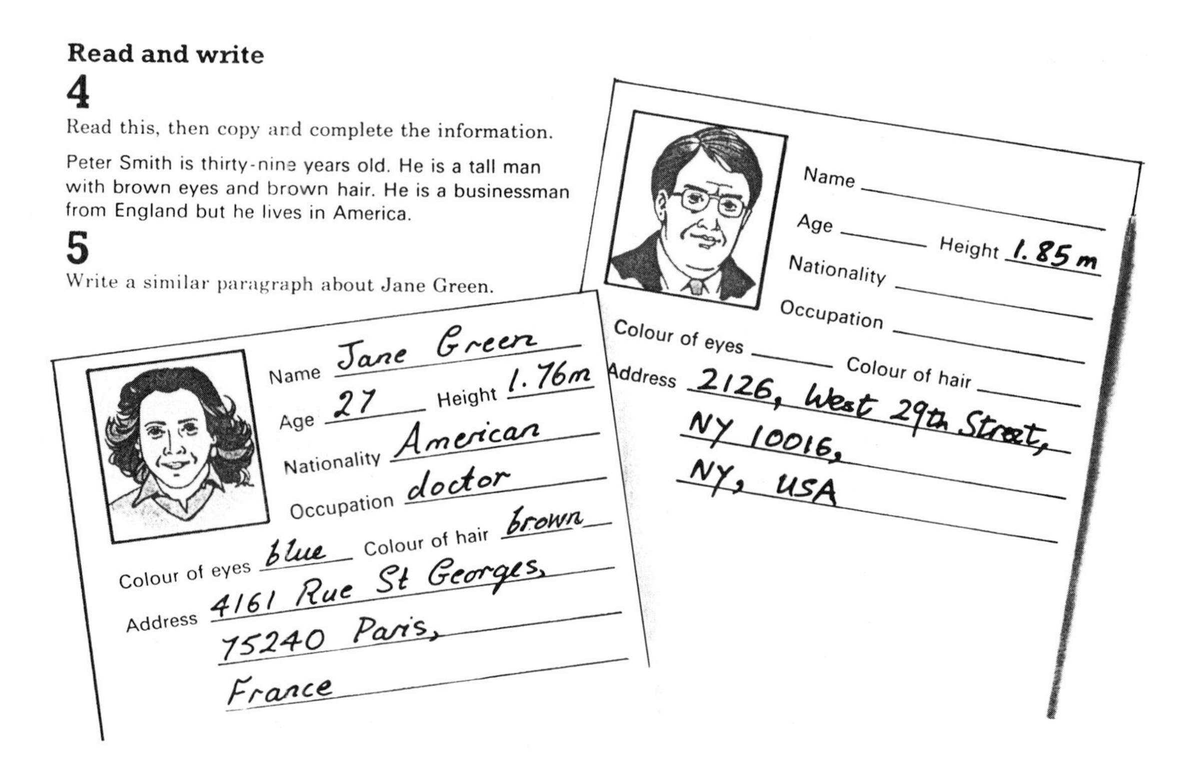

**Read and write**

**4**

Read this, then copy and complete the information.

Peter Smith is thirty-nine years old. He is a tall man with brown eyes and brown hair. He is a businessman from England but he lives in America.

**5**

Write a similar paragraph about Jane Green.

Name Jane Green
Age 27 Height 1.76m
Nationality American
Occupation doctor
Colour of eyes blue Colour of hair brown
Address 4161 Rue St Georges, 75240 Paris, France

Name
Age Height 1.85 m
Nationality
Occupation
Colour of eyes Colour of hair
Address 2126, West 29th Street, NY 10016, NY, USA

(b)

Read about Switzerland:

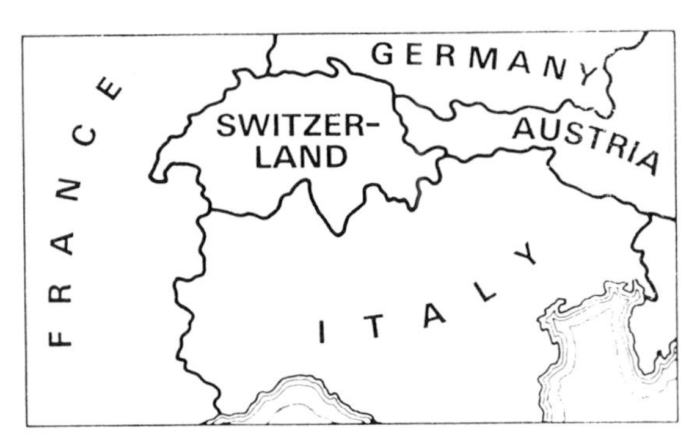


Switzerland is in Europe. It stands between Germany in the north, Austria in the east, Italy in the south and France in the west. About 5½ million people live in Switzerland and they speak French, German or Italian.

a) Now write about Austria. Use these notes:

north: Germany and Czechoslovakia / east: Hungary / south: Yugoslavia and Italy / west: Switzerland / 7 million / German

b) Now write about your own country.

4.3.3
Dictation as a reinforcement activity

The purpose of this short section is to indicate where dictation belongs in a writing programme. Clearly it differs from the reinforcement activities described above, because it involves listening and the ability to transform what is heard into its written form. However, since a dictation should be based on language with which the students are already familiar through other contexts (that is, it is essentially a re-presentation of known language items), it can be useful as an alternative reinforcement activity.

The difficulties which students have with this type of exercise should not be underestimated. An alternative approach to the 'conventional' dictation is to provide the students with an outline, in the form of an incomplete text, which they fill in from what they hear read aloud. This permits a more natural form of delivery, although less writing is involved. Texts used for dictation may also be in the form of notes and short letters, thus adding to the realism of the activity.

## 4.4 Sentence linking activities

Our goal through this type of activity is to begin to familiarise the students with the cohesive devices which are used in composing a text. They can then begin to combine structures which they have learned orally to form an acceptable sequence in writing. For this purpose, in order to make any headway, it will be necessary to introduce a selected number of linking devices and to practise these through writing. A *basic kit* at this stage might consist of the following:

| | |
|---|---|
| *Co-ordinators* | and, but, or, so |
| *Conjunctions* | although, when, until, so that (etc.) |
| *Sequencers* | then, after that, meanwhile, first, next, finally |
| *Linkers* | moreover, however, therefore, as a result, in fact, of course, on the other hand, etc. |

Some procedures for practising these are suggested below. Although this should normally be done within the context of a text, such as a letter, this does not preclude some initial practice for the purpose of familiarising the students with linking *sentences*, as in the first example below.

(a)

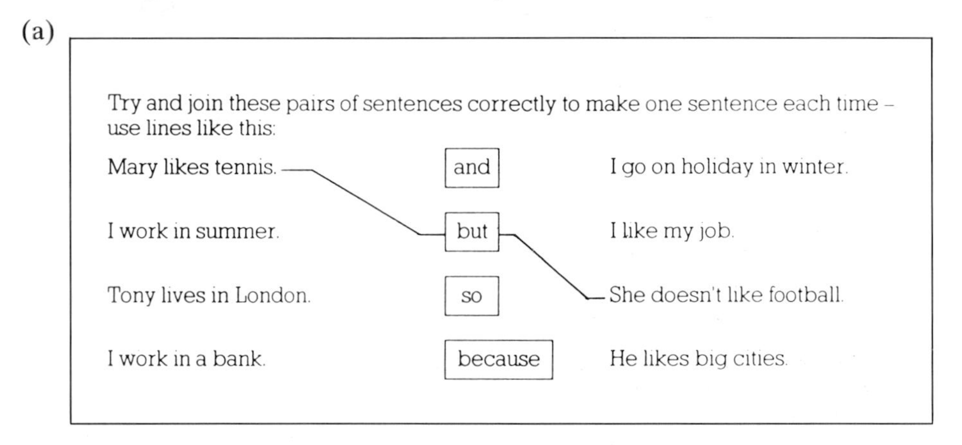
Try and join these pairs of sentences correctly to make one sentence each time – use lines like this:

| | | |
|---|---|---|
| Mary likes tennis. | and | I go on holiday in winter. |
| I work in summer. | but | I like my job. |
| Tony lives in London. | so | She doesn't like football. |
| I work in a bank. | because | He likes big cities. |

The students then have to write four *true* sentences about themselves.

(b) *The students complete a short text, using suitable linking words or phrases from a given list.*

For example:

*Complete the letter below. Use suitable words or phrases from this box*:

| | | | |
|---|---|---|---|
| although | and | by the way | so that |
| also | because | however | that |
| and | but | so | that |

Notice that 'exercises' like these, in the form of a complete text, also serve to introduce the student to such points as the layout of a letter, different modes of address and salutation, etc. Examples of these should be written up on the board and the students asked to copy them into their notebooks for reference. It is important, therefore, to incorporate a range of such features which will be useful to the students when they themselves are asked to write letters (as communication tasks, for example).

99 North Road
Bloxley
October 7 19..

Dear Tom,

I am sending you my new address, ... you can write to me. Of course I... hope ... you will come... stay with us soon.

I like our new house,... it is very noisy... it is near a main road. ..., my bedroom is at the back of the house,... I don't hear any noise at night. ... my sister's room is at the front... she says... she can't sleep! ..., she sends you her best wishes. Write soon. I am looking forward to hearing from you. All the best.

Yours,
Alan

(c) *The students complete a text by inserting clauses and sentences from a jumbled list of items (see (b) page 34) in the correct places.*

For example, the 'outline' for the second paragraph in the letter above could be presented as follows:

. . . . . . . . . ., although . . . . . . . . . . because . . . . . . . . . . . . .
However, . . . . . . . . . ., so . . . . . . . . . . But . . . . . . . . . . and
. . . . . . . . . . that . . . . . . . . . . By the way, . . . . . . . . . . . . . .

**4.5 Communication activities**

Throughout this stage, while writing activities are still to a large extent serving to reinforce oral work and while the foundation for writing skills is still being laid (as indicated in 4.1.2), it is nevertheless important to show the students that writing can be used for the purpose of communication. The activities which we set up for this purpose are necessarily simple in form and limited in scope but they will serve to motivate the students towards learning how to express themselves through writing. Some examples are given below.

(a) *The students write instructions which other students in the class (or the teacher!) have to carry out.*

For example:

> Take your exercise book and put it on top of the cupboard.

> Go and hold George's hand!

They may also be asked to write a sequence of instructions to be carried out. This is a useful device for practising items such as *First . . . Next . . . After that, . . .* For example:

> First go to the front of the class. Then write something on the blackboard. After that, clean the blackboard.

These instructions may be given to anyone in the class to perform. Alternatively, they may be addressed to someone by name, in the form of a note or short letter. For example:

Dear Ann, Wednesday

Draw a picture of a monkey! It's sitting on a box and it's wearing a big hat.

Yours,
Fred

PS It's a big monkey!

Activities along these lines are particularly useful for practising structures and items of vocabulary which have recently been taught for oral purposes.

(b) *The students write to one another to ask for information.*

Who's your favourite singer?

Which month were you born in?



The student who gets one of these requests can simply write the information on the same piece of paper. This enables the activity to go at a much faster pace — which is part of the fun!

(c) *Ask the students to write short messages to one another in the form of a note or short letter.*

For example:

Dear Mary,

I like your new dress. Where did you buy it?

Yours,
Ann

These 'messages' must be *answered* by the students to whom they are addressed. For example:

> Dear Ann,
>
> Thank you for your note. I bought the dress at 'Corn Poppy.' By the way, I like your new sweater. How much did it cost?
>
> Yours,
> Mary

This activity can quickly generate a flow of correspondence round the class.

(d) *Ask the students to write short letters to one another which involve some form of roleplay.*

For example, they may send one another invitations to a party, together with a request to bring certain items. Relevant language may be written on the board as a guide. For example: *Would you like to . . .? Will you please bring . . .?*

> Dear Fred,
>
> Would you like to come to my party on Saturday June 9? It starts at eight o'clock.
>
> If you can come, will you please bring six plates, four glasses and some records.
>
> Best wishes,
> Yours,
> Mary

As with the 'messages' in (c), these invitations must be *answered*. The person to whom they are addressed can accept the invitation or decline to come, giving his reasons. If he accepts the invitation, he should say whether he can bring all the items requested or only some of them. The activity may be extended to include giving or asking for directions to get to somebody's house.

## 4.6 Writing for fun

The activities in this section are not intended to help develop the learners' composition skills — because as a rule they will not be writing a text in a conventional sense. For the most part they will be writing things — questionnaires, puzzles, programmes, for example — which they can *do something with*. Usually they will be working together, in pairs or small groups, and this will involve talking as well as writing. Students usually enjoy these activities because they see the point of doing them, like those in the previous section, and also because in a small way, even at this elementary level, they get the opportunity to express themselves imaginatively.

(a) *Writing questionnaires*

The students, preferably working in pairs, write questionnaires which they can use to interview one or more other students in the class. Notice the various types of questionnaire.

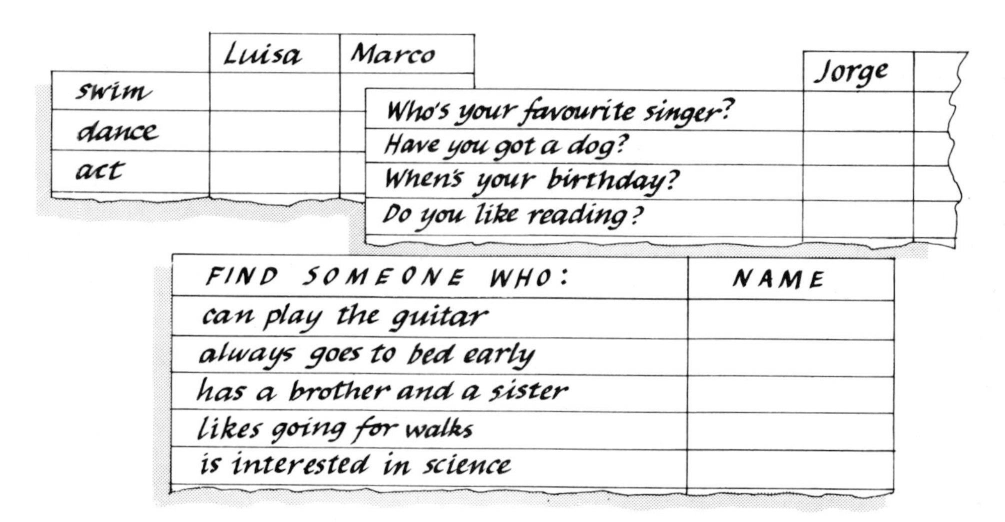


Questionnaires can focus on specific topics and even particular items of language. This need not make the activity less enjoyable.

(b) *Writing quizzes*

Students enjoy writing questions, in the form of a short quiz, on a text they have just read (as an alternative to 'comprehension questions' in the book!). They should work in small groups for this and then exchange their quizzes with another group.

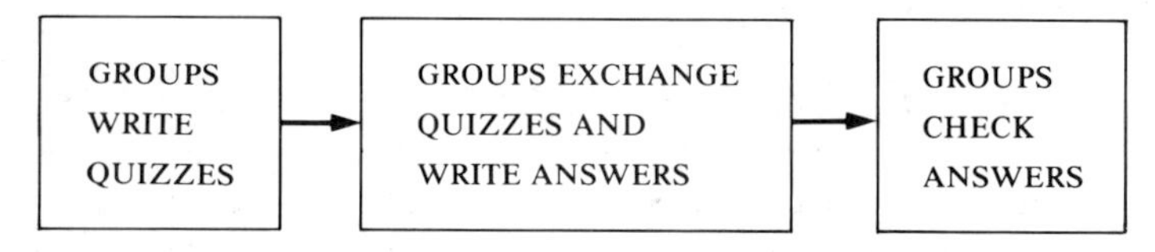


In the same way they can write quizzes which involve remembering or looking for information given in previous units in the coursebook (a useful form of revision!) or 'general knowledge' quizzes.

| | |
|---|---|
| 1 How old is Buck? | |
| 2 Can Penny speak Spanish? | |
| 3 What does SOS mean? | |
| 4 How m | |

| | |
|---|---|
| 1 What's the capital of France? | |
| 2 What language do they speak in Brazil? | |
| 3 Can birds see colours? | |

(c) *Writing puzzles*

The students, working individually or in pairs, write one or more puzzles like these, which they give to other students to answer.

WHAT IS IT?
It lives in the sea. It has ten arms.
It does not have any bones. It is not a fish!

In the same way, students can write 'secret messages' for one another in some kind of code, which other students have to interpret.

CANY OUCO MEAN DSEE MEAT ELEV ENOC LOCK?

ICAN TCOM EATE LEVE NOCL OCKI CANS EEYO UATE IGHT.

(d) *Writing programmes*

The students, working in groups to share their ideas, write a TV/radio programme to cover a possible evening's entertainment. Each student then makes his own copy of the programme, which can be used for pairwork activities, such as telling your partner what you saw or listened to the previous evening or agreeing which programmes to watch or listen to that evening.

Rad
6.0
6.15
7.15
8.0

TV Channel 1
6.0 News
Sports Report
6.30 Science: The Sun
7.0 Film: The World of Dreams
8.30 Quiz

(e) *Writing jumbled texts*

The students work in pairs or small groups to write a dialogue or a four-to five-sentence story sequence, which they then cut up into separate sentences and give to another pair or group to put together.

(f) *Writing role descriptions*

Normally, when we want students to do a roleplay activity, we *give* them a description of the role we want them to play. However, even at an elementary level the students can write simple role descriptions for one another. Incidentally, they involve little use of cohesive devices.

Give the students pictures (male or female faces) as a stimulus and a list of the items to be included (e.g. name, age, nationality, job, interests, etc.). Each student writes a role description for one other specific student in the class. This is important because it adds to the fun: the students usually write in some unusual features for the partner they have chosen or been given!

(g) *Writing mystery stories*

For this activity the students are given a series of questions which they must answer in order. For example: *Who was the person? Where was s/he? What was s/he doing? What did s/he say? What did s/he do after that?* Each student then takes it in turns to answer a question. When the first student has answered his question, he folds the paper over so that the next student cannot see what he has written (and so on). When all the questions have been answered, the students unfold the sheet of paper and read their mystery story.

(h) *Writing imaginary diaries*

THE PRIME MINISTER'S DIARY

MONDAY I am not well today!
I did not sleep well last night. I had a bad dream - about a bomb.

FRIDAY The people do not like me! And I don't like the people!
I am going to run away - to America! My plane will come at

The students may of course be asked to keep *real* diaries — at this stage or perhaps slightly later on in the course, but they will not want and should not be asked to show these to one another. On the other hand, writing the imaginary diary for a famous person of their choice or for a fictitious character is something they will be willing to share and will very likely stimulate their imaginations. The students should work in pairs or groups (although this is an activity they could equally well do on their own). They may like to continue writing about their character from time to time.

(i) *Writing about pictures*

This is an activity especially intended to stimulate the imagination and self expression. The students will need a picture showing a situation that is likely to suggest different interpretations. Ask them to talk about their picture and to decide what the situation is about. Then get them to write down their ideas — without worrying too much about sentence connection. They should then compare their ideas with those of another group.

I want a big one!

Instead of pictures, you can use speech bubbles drawn on the board. For example, about this one the students might write: *A boy is in a shop. He wants an icecream. His mother buys one but it is small. So he says: "........"*

## 4.7 Writing in class

The activities in the last two sections are intended to be done in class. Some could even take up a fair amount of time. This should require no justification because generally the students are also talking. However, the important thing is that activities of this kind change students' attitudes towards writing: they come to see how they can communicate through writing; how they can use writing purposefully and how it forms a natural part of certain activities. In addition to this, you can also work *with* the students either collaborating with them on a task or joining in an activity (e.g. *you* should also write to your students and get them to write to you for the activities in 4.5; *you* can also write questionnaires, quizzes, etc.). You will also get opportunities to check their work informally while the activity is still fresh in their minds. This is very different from the typical teacher role of correcting homework!

**Discussion**

1 Reread 4.1.1 and 4.1.2. What advice would you give a fellow teacher (or intending teacher) about setting up writing activities in the early stages?
2 From your own experience, do you agree that copying is an aid to retention in language learning?
3 From your own experience of learning to write in a foreign language, do you think enough attention was paid to activities:
(a) to practise linking sentences and sequencing ideas;
(b) to show how you can communicate through writing;
(c) to show how writing can be enjoyable?
4 What is your view of the value of dictation as a writing activity?

**Exercises**

1 Examine any coursebook to see what provision it makes for the presentation and practice of linking devices in the early stages.
2 Examine any coursebook to see what provision it makes for meaningful copying.
3 Devise a parallel writing activity, for use in the early stages, similar to those in 4.3.2.
4 Devise an exercise in linking sentences, for use in the early stages, similar to the one in 4.4 (b).
5 Suggest a writing activity, to be used in the early stages, which could be based on this map.

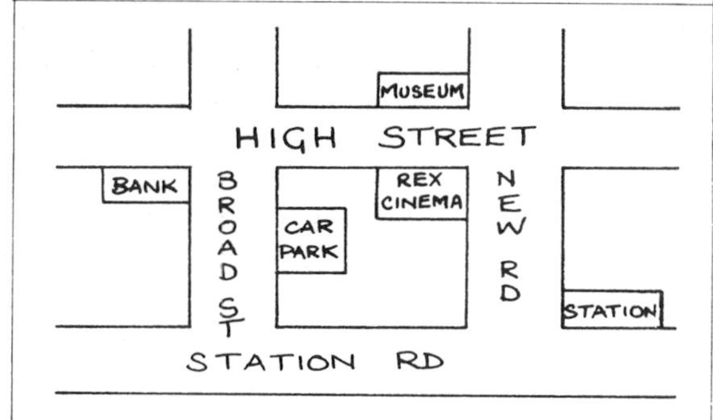


6 Devise an activity which could be used in the early stages to let the learners enjoy writing.

**References**

1 On the importance of getting the learners to evaluate one another's writing see C Brumfit in S Holden (ed.) (1983).
2 For writing in the early stages, see G Abbott and P Wingard (1981) Ch.6; J Harmer (1983) pages 65–75; P Hubbard et al (1983) pages 61–71 and A Pincas (1982a) pages 18–21 and 91–101.
3 For examples of writing activities in the early stages see T Hedge (1983a); A Pincas (1982b) and L Woods (1986).
4 Examples of writing activities in this chapter have been taken from J Harmer: *Meridian* (Longman 1985) (4.3.2 (a)); L Woods: *Writing 1* (Cassell 1986) (4.4 (a)) and M Palmer and D Byrne: *Track* (Longman 1982) (4.2.2 (d) and 4.3.2 (b)).

# 5

# Developing skills

## 5.1 The importance of demonstrating progress

At the post-elementary to intermediate level,* it is essential that, whatever the *scope* of the writing programme, it should not lose direction and momentum. This means that the writing programme must be *carefully planned* to develop a mastery of new skills, which the learners can use for a continually expanding range of tasks. At the same time, since writing will still be *guided* to a large extent, we need to make the activities as varied as possible, avoiding a monolithic approach which relies on a limited range of exercise types.

### 5.1.1 The main features of the writing programme

(a) *The writing programme should continue to provide opportunities for reinforcing language learned orally.*

At the same time, however, we may assume that the learners are being exposed to a greater amount of written language either through the type of texts in their coursebook or through supplementary reading. At this stage, therefore, the amount of dialogue writing should be gradually reduced, although it should not be abandoned altogether, partly because it is one way of getting the students to write material which they can use themselves — for oral work, for example — and partly because dialogue writing may be one of the requirements of the examination. However, as the main format for reinforcement practice at this level, we can now begin to make greater use of *informal letter-writing*, since this provides a convenient and appropriate way of re-presenting material learned orally and of course by this stage the learners are already familiar with this type of writing.

(b) *The writing programme should be designed to include a greater range of the resources of the written language.*

The basic kit, suggested in 4.4 should be expanded to incorporate, for

*90–225 hours or approximately the second and third years of a secondary school course. The suggestions in this chapter must be read in conjunction with Chapters 6 and 7 on the use of texts and visual material.

example, both a wider range of conjunctions used in compound and complex sentence structures and other linking devices. At the same time, we must increase the learners' awareness of rhetorical devices such as comparison and contrast, definition, exemplification, etc. (see the procedures suggested in 2.1.2) and their ability to use these. For this purpose, we should now begin to introduce a certain amount of institutional-type writing, such as formal letters and reports. As at the previous stage of the programme, when the students were introduced to writing informal letters, this component will *teach them something new through writing* and will therefore increase their interest and motivation.

(c) *The amount of control over what the learners write should be reduced.*

At this stage they should learn to respond to 'cues' which stimulate their imaginations but leave them relatively or completely free to decide *what* they actually write and how they organise their ideas.

(d) *The range of communication tasks should be extended.*

Thus, alongside the guided writing activities suggested in 5.2–5.4, the learners are also given opportunities for free expression. These will to some extent involve greater reliance on roleplay techniques.

5.1.2
The role of the teacher

It has been emphasised that this is a delicate and crucial stage of the writing programme. It is especially important, therefore, to:

(a) *Get the right balance of writing activities.*

For example, with regard to dialogue writing, this should be reduced considerably unless it is an examination requirement. At the same time, it is important to extend *systematically* the sentence linking and sequencing component of the programme described in 5.3. No real progress will be made unless this is done.

(b) *Ensure that the type of writing activity and the formats used to practise these are sufficiently varied so that the students do not get bored.*

Practice materials may have to be *selected and adapted* from a variety of sources.

(c) *Gauge carefully the amount of guidance required.*

It is likely that the amount of oral preparation for many writing activities can now be reduced. The amount of individual writing may also be increased, especially when the students approach the time when they will have to do a public written examination. For certain activities, however, it has been suggested that pair and group work will still be extremely valuable.

## 5.2 Reinforcement activities

The need to provide opportunities for practising what has been learned orally continues throughout this stage, although the increasing use of texts other than dialogues now makes it possible to introduce writing activities which are based more directly on a reading text (see Chapter 6). As we have noted, dialogue writing has almost outlived its usefulness as a writing activity and, if we continue to use it, we must look for fresh ways of presenting it to the learners.

The suggestions for reinforcement activities given below are classified according to the *type* of writing involved.

### 5.2.1 Dialogue writing

(a) *The students are given a model dialogue, together with cues for writing parallel versions.*

This task is much freer than the one in 4.3.1: it is guided rather than controlled and the students can *select* from the cues provided. In the example below, which focuses on offering advice, the students also have to modify the form of the cues (for example, they must use the *–ing* form after *How about . . .?*)*

*Read this dialogue*:

A: What's up, Mike?
B: I don't know what to do this evening.
A: Well, why don't you go to the club, then?
B: Oh, that's not much fun, is it?
A: Well, how about coming to the cinema with me?
B: Hm, *that* sounds like a much better idea!

*Now choose any of these ideas (or use ones of your own) to write similar dialogues*:

| | |
|---|---|
| go and see (Jane) | go for a walk |
| help me cook the supper | sit and read the paper |
| have a game of cards | write some letters |
| help me wash the car | go and watch television |

(b) *The students are given an incomplete dialogue, together with instructions for completing it. These do not specify the actual words to be used.*

*Complete this dialogue*:

A: ................. (*Suggest doing something*)
B: Oh, all right. If that's what you really want to do.
A: ................. (*Enquire about B's wishes*)
B: Don't know. Go to the cinema, perhaps.
A: ................. (*Object to this idea*)
B: Oh, all right, then. Let's .................

*Now write (2) similar dialogues of your own.*

(c) *The students write the complete dialogue. They are given an outline or 'map' of the dialogue, but none of the actual words to be used.*

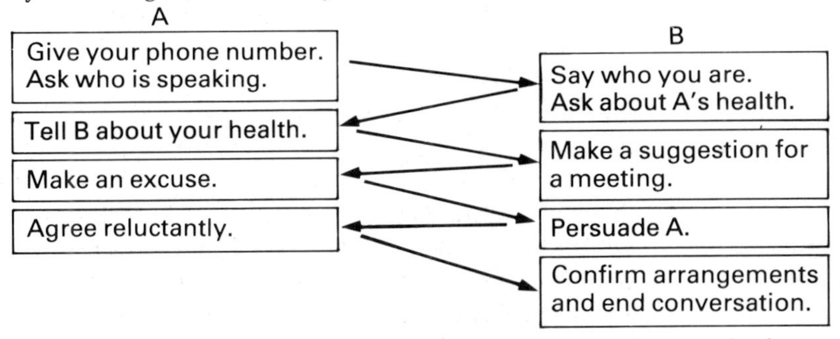


*As for Chapter 4, it should be kept in mind that the language used in the examples does not relate to any particular course.

Another possibility is to give the students a 'scenario'.

> Mr A has an appointment with Mr B in a big office block. When he enters the building, he announces his arrival to the receptionist, who speaks to Mr B on the phone. The receptionist then tells Mr A how to get to Mr B's office. Mr A gets out of the lift on the wrong floor. He meets an employee, who offers to take him to Mr B's office. When he gets there, Mr A, who is now rather late, makes his excuses and explains what happened.

It may be felt that this is rather a long way round to get the students to write a dialogue but remember at this stage we are looking for ways of providing *guidance without control*. Both the dialogue 'maps' and 'scenarios' direct the students towards certain uses of language, and thus prevent the production of rambling and often trivial dialogues, but at the same time require them to think of the actual words which will fit the situation. When they translate the scenarios into dialogue form, they can also write some narrative commentary in the form of stage directions. It should be noted that both dialogue 'maps' and 'scenarios' can be used at different levels of language attainment, depending on the sophistication of the task involved.

(d) *The students write a dialogue for which the setting is defined and some suggestions are given for the language to be used.*

For example:

*You are in a restaurant with a friend. You are looking at the menu, trying to decide what to have. Write the conversation you have. You may use these phrases:*

| | |
|---|---|
| How about . . .? | That's (rather) . . . |
| What shall we have to . . .? | I wonder what . . . |
| Have you ever . . .? | Why don't we . . . |
| This looks . . . | Let's ask . . . |

For activities (b) to (d), it is suggested that the students should be allowed to collaborate, either in pairs or in small groups, at least for the initial stage of the activity, when various possible forms of expression can be discussed. Thus, the students 'talk over' the dialogue together, work out a rough version and then, if they wish, each produce their own final version.

### 5.2.2 Writing notes and letters

By this stage the students are already familiar with writing informal letters, but there are various things we can do to give this activity a new slant. For example, we can teach new ways of beginning and ending letters. We can also see that the students are given systematic opportunities to practise writing letters which have, overall, a specific function such as making an apology (a complaint, an excuse), sending congratulations, giving directions, etc., and at the same time show how such tasks will require very different uses of language on different occasions and in particular how these depend on the relationship between the writer and the person he is addressing.

(a) *The students are given a model text, together with cues for writing parallel versions.*

This is similar to 5.2.1 (a). The cues may be phased out so that the students produce their own versions. For example:

*Read the following. It is an extract from a letter.*

Dear John,

. . . . . .

That reminds me - you asked my advice about buying a car. Personally, if I were you, I'd get a good second-hand one. But don't go to one of those big firms. Try to get one from someone who wants to sell his car privately. Make sure that there's nothing wrong with it, of course! In fact you should get a mechanic to look at it for you. . . . . .

(i) *Use these notes to write a letter to a friend who wants advice about a holiday*:
go to ................./do not stay in the town itself/find a quiet hotel just outside the town/get a room with a good view/make a booking as early as possible.

(ii) *Use these notes to write a letter to a friend who wants advice about how to find a new job*:
try to get a job with a new firm/do not go to an agency/buy a paper which has ads for jobs/.................

(iii) *Write a letter to a friend who wants advice about how to learn (a foreign language).*

(b) *The students are given an incomplete text, with suggestions or instructions about how to complete it.*

This activity can be particularly useful for practising specific items of language, such as the *–ing* form, as in the example below.

*You are introducing yourself to a penfriend. Complete this letter with reference to your own likes and dislikes, etc.*

Now I'd like to tell you something about myself. One of the things I like doing most (when I have time!) is . . . . . I'm also very fond of . . . . . and I quite like . . . . . as well, although I'm not very good at it. On the other hand, I'm not very interested in either . . . . . or . . . . . nor do I really like . . . . . As for . . . . . , I absolutely hate it!

(c) *The students complete a text by expanding notes.*

The notes in this example are within the framework of a letter, the theme of which is assumed to relate to a topic explored through a lesson in the coursebook.

*Complete this letter. Use the notes to write the second and third paragraphs.*

> Dear Jack,
>
> I hear you are changing your job shortly. I have a suggestion! Why don't you come and live with us? At the moment there are four of us sharing this flat, but one person is leaving at the end of the month.
>
> large flat / four bedrooms / one big living-room / kitchen etc / near centre of town
>
> arrangements as follows / share all expenses / for example ..... / buy own food
>
> It all works out very well. And of course there's one great advantage: you can do what you like here. Let me know about it as soon as possible.
>
> Yours,
> Bob

Activities like those suggested in (b) and (c) lend themselves well to *related* writing tasks within the context already established. For example, the students may be asked to write a short reply to Bob's letter based on cues like the following:

*Write back to say that you are interested in Bob's proposal but ask for more information about the following points*:
— how much is the rent?
— what other expenses are there?
— what arrangements are there for having guests?
— is it easy to find parking near the flat?
— who are the other people in the flat?

(d) *The students write the complete text. They are given guidance for the content but not for the language to be used.*

For example:
*You bought a bottle of perfume or after-shave lotion after seeing an advertisement for it. It gave you a skin complaint. Write a letter to the firm which made the product, saying*:
— what you bought (invent a suitable name)
— where you saw the advertisement and what the advertisement claimed (e.g. good for the skin)
— why you bought a very large bottle
— how it affected your skin
— what the doctor said
— why you want your money back

### 5.2.3 Writing short reports

The students may also be given a guided introduction to writing reports. For this, guidance should focus chiefly on the organisation and orderly presentation of ideas.

(a) *As a preliminary step, the students complete forms similar to this one.*

A penfriend agency has sent you this form. Complete it with details about yourself.

**Penfriend Service**
Reg. Office: 29 Bolsover Street, London W.1.

Please write legibly. Items 1-6 should be completed in capital letters.

1 Name ______
2 Age ______
3 Sex ______
4 Nationality ______
5 Religion ______
6 Occupation ______
7 Education ______
8 How long have you been learning English? ______
9 Where did you learn it? ______
10 Have you ever visited England? ______
11 If so, give details ______
12 Brief statement of interests and hobbies ______
13 Reason(s) for wanting a penfriend ______
14 Details of type of penfriend required ______

(b) *The students are given a model text, together with cues for writing parallel versions.*

*Read this short report*:

Alan is very practical, *but* he is *also* rather untidy. *For example*, he is very good at repairing things, such as bikes, *but* he never puts his tools away afterwards.

*Now write similar reports, using these adjectives or others of your own choice*:

| | | | |
|---|---|---|---|
| careless | hard working | lazy | rude |
| clever | kind | nice | silly |

The students may also be given outlines and asked to write reports on other students in the class. For example:

. . . (NAME) is very . . . and as a rule (he) is also . . . . For example, . . . . On the other hand, (he) can be . . . and sometimes (he) is also . . . .

The information for reports may also be derived from completed forms, similar to the one in (a).

(c) *The students are given a model text and, after focused practice (e.g. identifying advantages and disadvantages) are asked to write a parallel one.*

Look at the details of these two beaches. Write a report about which beach would be suitable for a new hotel. Use *although* and *because*.

| | ADVANTAGES | DISADVANTAGES |
|---|---|---|
| Smuggler's Bay | beautiful<br>easy to get to | very rough sea<br>small beach |
| Sunset Beach | long sandy beach<br>calm sea | rather flat<br>no main road |

**5.3 Sentence linking and sequencing activities**

It has been suggested that this component of the writing programme should be extended and strengthened by varying the formats for practice to include formal letters (for this the students must be given appropriate models) and reports, and by expanding the basic kit of linking devices. This may be done by drawing systematically on the items in the Appendix. Suggestions for activities are given below.

(a) *The students complete a short text by using suitable linking words or phrases.*

We can use this type of exercise for various purposes. First, to *familiarise* the students with a wider range of linking devices from the expanded basic kit. After this, they may be asked to *select from a list* which is more extensive than the number of items omitted from the text. Finally, they may be asked to *supply their own linking devices*. An example from the second stage (i.e. choosing from a more extensive list) is given below.

*Use suitable linking devices from the box to complete the text below*:

| | | | |
|---|---|---|---|
| also | but | incidentally | not only |
| although | but also | in particular | on the other hand |
| and | for | in this way | since |
| and | for the moment | instead | therefore |
| because | however | meanwhile | too |

Janet West's sister is an air hostess for a famous international airline, . . . Janet wants to become one . . . . . . ., she is still too young: the minimum age for an air hostess is twenty. . . . Janet is only just over sixteen.

. . . she has taken a job in an office. . . . she . . . attends evening classes. . . ., she wants to improve her French and Spanish, . . . foreign languages are an essential qualification for an air hostess.

. . ., Janet is gaining experience through her present job. . . . the office where she works is a travel agency. . . . she is learning . . . how to deal with people . . . quite a lot about the places she one day hopes to visit.

Again the students may be asked to do these tasks in pairs or in small groups, so that they can discuss the various possibilities. It should be emphasised that there need be no one correct version. What is important is that, if the students choose an item which did not appear in the original version, they should consider whether this affects the meaning of the text and if so, in what way.

At this stage we may also use incomplete texts to get the students to consider other semantic links through grammar and lexis. For example, the first paragraph of the text above might be presented with the following items omitted.

> Janet West's sister is an air hostess for a famous international . . ., and Janet wants to become . . . too. At the moment, . . . is still too young: . . . for an air hostess is twenty and . . . is only just over sixteen.

All the items omitted — *airline, one, she, the minimum age, Janet*, which would appear as part of a much longer list, are ones which contribute to the grammatical and lexical cohesion of the text.

(b) *The students combine sentences so that they form an acceptable sequence.*

The linking devices to be used may either be provided or the students may be asked to supply their own. For example:

*Join these sentences in any suitable way so that they form a sequence. Use 'she' in place of 'Janet' where appropriate.*

1 Janet is gaining experience through her present job.
2 Janet works in a travel agency.
3 Janet is learning how to deal with people.
4 Janet is learning quite a lot about the places she one day hopes to visit.

(c) *The students rewrite texts within the framework of a related outline.*

For example:

*Read this text. Then complete the text below so that the same ideas are expressed in a different way:*

> There are two sides to the work of stuntmen. They actually do most of the things you see on the screen. For example, they jump from high buildings. However, they do not fall onto hard ground but onto empty cardboard boxes covered with a mattress.

The work of stuntmen . . . to it. They actually do almost . . . which you see them . . ., such as . . . . But instead of . . ., they . . . onto cardboard boxes which . . . .

(d) *The students form texts from a list of jumbled sentences.*

See 4.3.1 (c), where the students formed a dialogue in this way, and 4.6 (e), where they wrote their own texts. While the purpose of this activity is to get the students to *think* about sentence sequencing, it must not become just a puzzle. Narrative texts usually have a fairly transparent sequence and therefore provide a good starting point. You can provide some framework of reference, as with the map in the activity below. As a final stage, use expository texts with a clear opening 'topic' sentence. Otherwise the first sentence should be indicated.

*Look at the map. John lives at 7, Elm Lane. He's having a party. What directions must he give to his friends? Put these instructions in the right order. Number them 1 to 7.*

| | |
|---|---|
| | Walk along until you get to the library. |
| | Walk around the pond to Hazelbank Road. |
| 1 | Get off the bus at The Green Man. |
| | Turn right into Elm Lane. |
| | Turn right into Firtree Lane. |
| | Number 7 is on the left. |
| | Go over the bridge. |

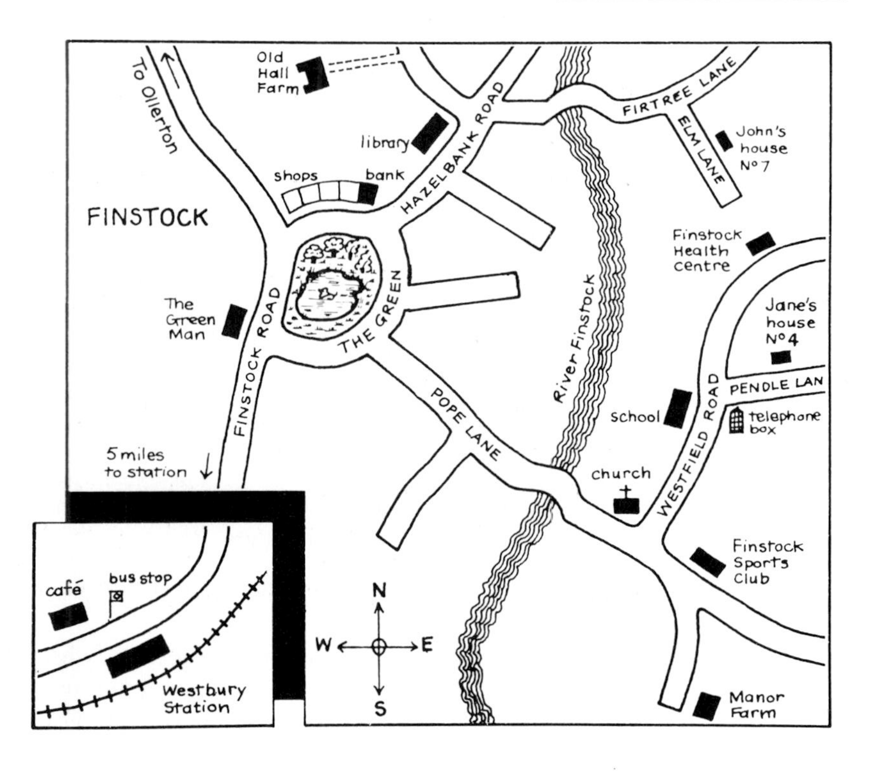

The students can be given a diagram which shows how the ideas in the text have been organised. For the activity below, the students have already seen a parallel text.

Here is a plan of the first paragraph in Exercise 1. Use these sentences to write a paragraph about London with the same plan.

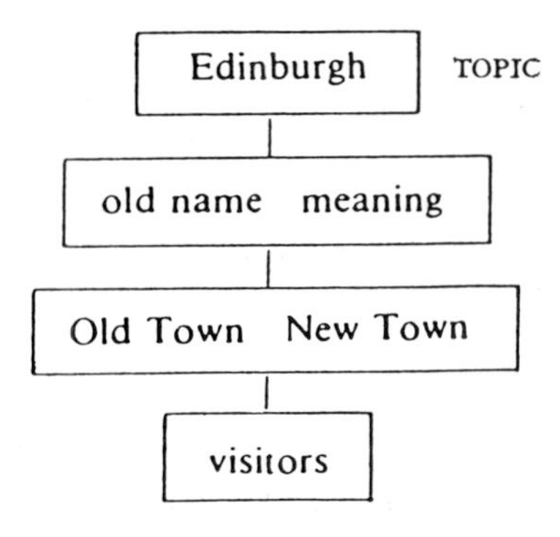


**a** The East End has a lot of charm, with small narrow streets and old grey buildings.
**b** London is England's capital city.
**c** It is very different from the West End, with its large expensive shops and lovely green parks.
**d** Its old name was *Londinium*.
**e** London has many shops, restaurants and theatres and offers a lot to visitors.
**f** This means the village of the bold man.

Sentences can be broken down into clauses to draw further attention to the logical structure of a text. For example:

*Use these sentences to write a paragraph about the pygmies. Change the order and add any necessary punctuation.*

They can move easily in the forest
and they are not afraid of it
The forest in the centre of Africa is a dangerous place
Pygmies know the forest well
because they are very small
A big pygmy is only lm 40cm tall
but the pygmies are happy there

(e) *The students do exercises which specifically direct their attention to the way ideas are organised in a text.*

This may be done in a guided form at the start, with the help of information presented in tabular form, together with examples of the kind of text which the students are required to write. For example:

*Study the two texts, which are based on information given in the table. Then write similar texts of your own, to form part of a letter telling someone how to get to a place.*

| *Destination* | *Alternatives* 1 | 2 | *Time for 1* |
|---|---|---|---|
| airport | coach | taxi | ½ hour |
| sports ground | tube | bus | 10 mins |
| motor show | taxi | tube | 5 mins |
| theatre | on foot | taxi | ¼ hour |
| hospital | bus | on foot | * |
| port | boat | bus | * |

*Use any suitable period of time

You can go to the airport either by coach or by taxi. If you go by coach, it takes at least half an hour. By taxi, on the other hand, it takes only ten minutes. For that reason, I suggest the second possibility.

There are two ways of getting to the sports ground: either by tube or by bus. By tube it only takes ten minutes, while if you go by bus, on the other hand, it may take you over twenty minutes. My advice to you, then, is to go by tube.

(f) *The students write texts based on a model that has a clear logical development.*

This may be shown through a diagram. For example:

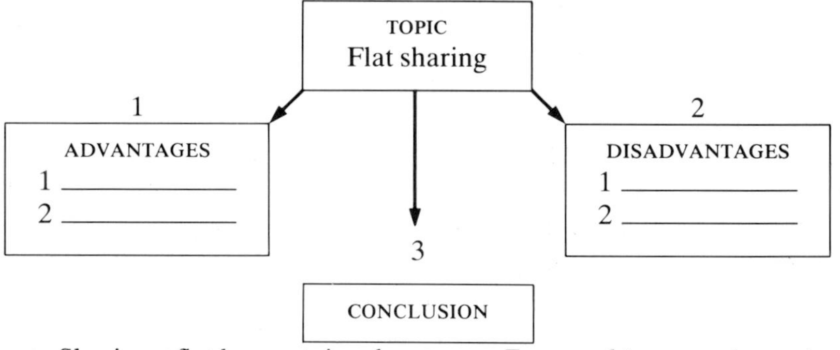


Sharing a flat has certain advantages. *For one thing*, you do not have to do all the housework yourself. *Besides*, it is also cheaper. *On the other hand*, you may not have much privacy and, moreover, it may be noisy. All in all, it is probably better to live on your own!

The students are then given topics which can be written about within a similar framework. For example:

1 Living in a big city
2 Owning a car
3 Working in an office
4 Being a housewife

## 5.4 Reproduction exercises

These resemble dictations, in that the students have to listen to a text which is read aloud to them. However, instead of being asked to take this down segment by segment, which makes dictation a somewhat artificial exercise, they listen to the complete text a number of times (usually three or more) before they are asked to write. They are then required to 'reproduce' the text they have heard as accurately as possible, but they may fill in with their own words where their memory of the original fails them.

Like dictation, this type of activity also involves careful listening and the transformation of what is heard into its written form. However, it focuses much more on grasping the overall meaning of a text and in particular how one sentence relates to another. We can also make our own 'rules' for this activity. For example, the students may be allowed to make brief notes during the final reading. Alternatively, we may write key words and phrases on the board, to remind the students of some of the main ideas. In either case, we thus ensure that the activity does not become just a test of memory. We may also write a framework of linking words and sequencing devices on the board, so that in effect we give the students a structural 'skeleton' around which the text can be 'reproduced'.

## 5.5 Communication activities

At this stage, it is important that communication activities should match the growing ability of the learners to express themselves through the written form of the language. They should, therefore, in the first instance be on a much more *extensive* scale, compared with the modest tasks of sending messages and notes (see 4.5. This *type* of activity, however, where the students write to one another in the class can still be used provided that they are asked to produce something more substantial.). They must also be *more challenging*. With this type of writing activity, the students may of course make mistakes, as with free oral expression, but the important thing, from the point of view of motivation, is to demonstrate that writing is a purposeful activity.

April 1 19..

Dear Kate,

Would you like to ..... (+ activity) on ..... (+ day). If you can come, please meet me..... (+ place and time). You can't miss it, by the way. ..... (+exact location).

Looking forward to seeing you!

Ben

PS Don't be late!

You should also encourage and help the students to find penfriends as a way of extending communication practice. From time to time you can also conduct all or part of the lesson entirely through the medium of writing so that the students really appreciate what is involved in giving and receiving instructions, requests, etc. in this way.

In the activities below, more use is now made of roleplay, although not to the exclusion of other activities where the students write *as themselves*. The list of suggestions below, which is intended to indicate *typical activities* rather than to be exhaustive, frequently involves some form of collaboration in the writing task.

5.5.1
Roleplay activities

(a) *The Estate Agency*

Divide the class into two. Sub-divide one half into three or four groups, depending on the size of the class. Tell each of these groups that they represent an estate agency. They should also find a name for their agency. Their immediate task is to devise a form on which they can record information about the houses or flats which their 'clients' will give them when they come to see them.

Tell the students in the other half of the class that they are people who want to sell their houses and to buy another.

Each of them should write some notes describing the house they want to sell. It may be the house they actually live in or an imaginary one. They should also have some idea of the house they would like to buy.

The 'clients' then choose which agency they want to go to. They are interviewed by a member of the agency and fill in the form, on the basis of which a final description of their house is worked out. These descriptions are then written up and displayed, and can be read by those who want to buy a house.

The activity may be repeated at a later stage with the roles reversed. Instead of estate agencies, secondhand car firms can be used as an alternative setting.

(b) *The Magazine Advice Column*

Write the names of a number of magazine 'advice columns' on the board. These should be discussed with the class so that they know what kind of 'problems' each one deals with.

Then ask all the students in the class to write to one of the advice columns, asking for help with a personal problem. They can do this anonymously if they prefer.

Divide the class into small groups, each one representing the staff of an advice column. Distribute the letters among the groups, making sure that no one gets his own letter, and ask them to write replies to these letters. These replies should then be given to the students who wrote to the column.

Alternatively, both the letters and replies may be written up as wall sheets, so that the whole class can read them.

(c) *The News Desk*

Ask each student in the class to write two or three items of news (real or imaginary). Each item should not be more than about 50–60 words long and duplicate copies should be made of each item.

Divide the class into groups, each representing a 'News Desk'. Distribute the items of news among the various desks (because they are in duplicate, more than one 'desk' will get the same item) and ask each group to edit their items so as to produce a news bulletin, which can then be read aloud to the class.

(d) *Job vacancies*

Distribute a list of 'job vacancies' in five or six big firms and ask each student to write a letter of application for one of these jobs (giving personal details, real or imaginary).

Divide the class into groups representing each of these firms and ask them to write their replies. In these, they should suggest a date and time for an interview or say that the vacancy has already been filled, etc.

(e) *Complaints*

Select from magazines a variety of ads for well-known products and paste these on to cards. Ask each student in the class to choose one of these ads and to write a letter of complaint about either the product or the ad to the firm concerned.

Divide the class into groups, each representing a big firm responsible for advertising a number of these products. Then distribute the letters to the appropriate firms and ask them to discuss and write their replies. These should be sent to the person who wrote the letter of complaint.

(f) *Campaigns*

Divide the class into groups and ask each group to decide on some action they would take to improve their town: for example, by pulling down a certain building; by providing a facility of some kind, such as a new swimming pool, or tennis courts; by widening a street, etc. Each group should then announce, in the form of a press report, what they propose to do.

Each student in the class is then invited to respond to one or more of these proposals: for example, by writing to the press; by writing, in collaboration with two or more other students, a public protest or a notice calling for a meeting to protest against the proposal, or by writing anonymous letters to the persons concerned with the proposal.

(g) *Notices*

Divide the class into groups. Ask each to draw up a notice on a given topic: for example, starting a pop group or club; starting a protest against . . .; raising funds for . . ., etc. At least two groups should work on the same task so that they can compare their notices.

(h) *Rules and regulations*

Divide the class into groups and ask each group to draw up a list of rules and regulations to control a certain situation: for example, safety precautions (fire, hygiene, etc.) for a holiday camp. After each group has finished drawing up its list of rules and regulations, ask them to compare these with those of other groups.

(i) *Market research*

Divide the class into groups. Ask each group to draw up a market research questionnaire for a certain product. Each student should then use one of these questionnaires to interview other students in the class.

5.5.2
Report writing activities

(a) *Our town*

Divide the class into groups. Give each group the task of describing one feature of their town. For example:

— places of interest
— good places to eat at
— entertainment facilities
— sports facilities
— local industries, etc.

Each group should write their description in such a way that the feature described sounds attractive to someone visiting the town. Each student should also make his own copy of the description.

Then form new groups, making sure that they contain at least one representative from each of the original groups, and ask them to write a full report on their town based on these descriptions. The report may be accompanied by a map showing the location of various places of interest, etc.

(b) *Public interviews*

Ask a student who is willing to be interviewed to come to the front of the class. Ask the other students to question him about some experience, pleasant or unpleasant which he has had, and to make notes.

Divide the students into groups, ask them to compare notes and to compile an account of what was said by combining various ideas. When the groups have finished writing their versions, these should be read aloud and compared.

(c) *Private interviews*

Ask each student in the class to interview another student about some experience which he has had, and to make notes. Each student should then write a *rough version* from his notes and show this to the person he interviewed before writing up the final version.

(d) *Book reports*

Ask each student to write a report on a book he has read. If there is a class library, he should choose a book from this and place the report he has written inside the book for the guidance of prospective readers. If there is no class library, the book reports may be circulated among the students in the class in a folder. Similarly, the students may be asked to report on new records or on films they have seen.

(e) *Noticeboard*

Ask the students to write ads or notices for things which they would like to sell or to buy. These should be pinned on the class noticeboard or circulated round the class in a folder. The noticeboard may also be used as the location for some of the activities suggested in 5.6, e.g. 'problems', graffiti, jokes, or simply 'hello' messages to other students in the class.

(f) *References*

Ask each student in the class to request at least two other students to write him a character reference. The various references should then be compared with one another.

(g) *Class wallsheet*

Ask each student to write a contribution for a class wallsheet — items of class news, items of general interest. Divide the class into three or four groups and ask them to edit the various contributions. They must also decide how these will be arranged on the wallsheet. These wallsheets, when completed, should be displayed for the other students to read.

## 5.6 Writing for fun

We can go on using many of the activities suggested for fun writing in Chapter 4. In fact it is important to do this because it demonstrates to the students how much more they can get out of an activity as their proficiency in the language increases. Amongst the activities suggested, it is especially important to go on using questionnaires and quizzes, jumbled texts, role descriptions (see also (d) below), imaginary diaries and writing about pictures and speech bubbles. For writing about pictures in particular we can begin to expect more than just a few sentences and ideas jotted down.

(a) *Posing problems*

The students, working in pairs or small groups, think up problem situations such as:

*What would you do if . . . . . (the school caught fire / you became Prime Minister tomorrow / you had to live without water for a month / . . . .)?*

*We need (£1,000) at once! Can you suggest some ways of getting or making money?*

They then send these problems to one or more other pairs or groups for their suggested solutions.

(b) *Writing clues for crosswords*

For this the students, working in pairs or small groups, are given a crossword puzzle (perhaps made up by another group) like the one here. They then have to write the 'clues' (which you would normally be given to complete the crossword puzzle). These can be literal, e.g. for *school*: *You go there to study*, or amusing, *A place where they try hard to teach you things*.

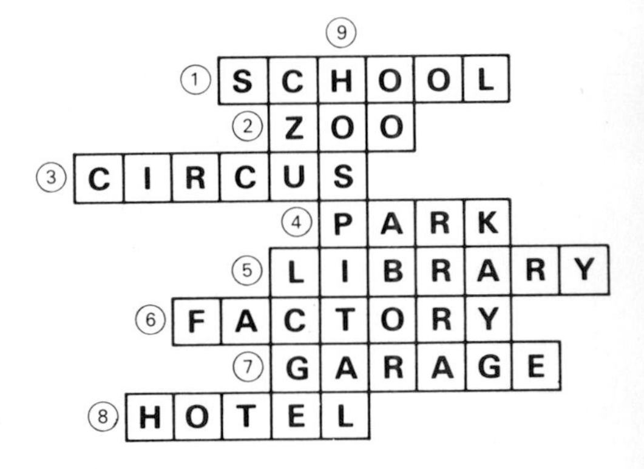


Alternatively, the 'clues' can consist of a series of sentences, e.g. *It's a very unpleasant place where they try to teach you things. It's like a kind of prison. You go there when you are (six) and you are 'free' when you are (sixteen). After that, it is usually difficult to get a job . . . . .*

(c) *Instructions for a game*

For the simple board game below, the students, working in groups, can write their own instructions for moving round the board. For example:

A If you have something to eat in your bag, go back 2 squares.

B If you went to bed before 10 o'clock last night, go forward 3 squares.

C Unless you know how to ride a bike, go back five squares.

To play this game, the students take it in turns to throw a dice, moving round the board first from left to right, then right to left (etc, following the arrows). When they land on a square, they look at the instructions (given in alphabetical order) to find out about their move. The first player to reach 'home' is the winner.

For this activity the students, therefore, have to write instructions for each letter of the alphabet on the board.

| | | | | | | | |
|---|---|---|---|---|---|---|---|
| START → | B | K | L | F | O | A | T ↓ |
| V ↓ | R | Q | X | C | H | L ← | P |
| Z → | F | O | J | Z | Y | D | S ↓ |
| A ↓ | N | W | K | C | X | V | P |
| I | F | M | T | Q | H | B | HOME |

(d) *Role descriptions*

This is a more advanced version of the activity described in 4.6 (f). The students have to produce descriptions which could be used for simple simulation situations (based perhaps on characters in the coursebook). The text involves more sentence linking and sequencing than the earlier activity, but is still a relatively straightforward piece of writing. Once again, the role description is intended for a specific person and should aim to be amusing.

> Your name is Jacky Snatcher. You lived in the village when you were a child. Your father was the shopkeeper and you didn't have much money. Now you are rich and you want to make a lot of changes. For example:
>
> A good hotel (Your husband likes drinking/....)
> A supermarket (You want to be able to shop quickly/.....)
> A big police station (You like to have a lot of policemen around/.... )

(e) *Scenarios*

The students, working in groups, write 'scenarios' like the one in 5.2.1 (c) or short stories which they give to one another to decide how to act out. Notice that the scenario has opportunities for talk but does not give any of the actual words. Thus we have an activity which develops as follows:

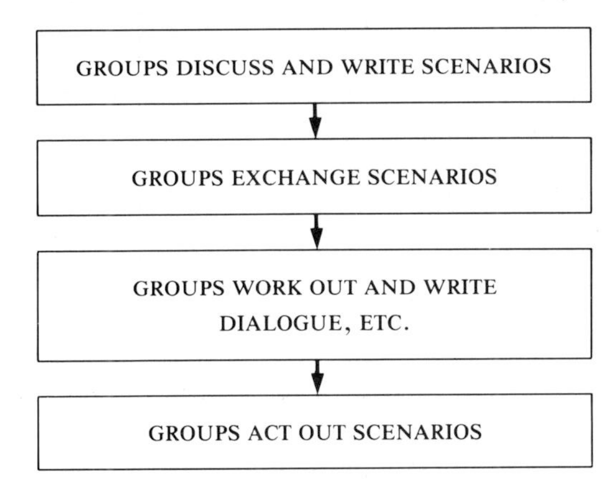


(f) *Inaccurate accounts*

The students, working in groups, write a description of a well-known person, place or thing or an account of an event which contains some deliberate mistakes of fact. The groups then exchange what they have written and try to detect the inaccuracies.

(g) *Jumbled stories*

This is similar to 4.6 (e), except that the students, working in groups, have to write two short stories of about four to six sentences each. The stories can be about the same person or a similar event. The stories are then cut up into separate sentences and given to another group to sort out into the two original stories.

TWO TALL STORIES

Make two stories with these sentences:

(a) The woman who was sitting behind the elephant couldn't see.

(b) "I'm not surprised," the elephant said. "The coffee's not very good."

(c) "He's read the book," the man said. "Now he wants to see the film."

(d) A man once took his elephant friend to the cinema.

(e) The waiter gave one to him and the elephant drank it.

(f) One day an elephant went into a café and asked for a cup of coffee.

(g) "Why have you brought this elephant in here?" she asked.

(h) "We don't see many elephants in here," the waiter said.

(h) *Jigsaw writing*

Cut up any suitable picture: it should have a clear overall structure and some, but not too much, detail. Give one such picture to each group and ask the students to work in pairs to work out a description of one or more pieces. They should not look at one another's pieces. When they have written out their descriptions, they should put away their pieces and try to work out what the picture as a whole looks like from what they have written. When they have described, orally or in writing, the complete picture, they can check this against the visual.

(i) *Instructions for drawing a map or picture*

The students, working in groups, have to draw a simple map or picture like the ones below. They then work out the step by step instructions for drawing these. For example, for the picture:

1 Draw two trees, one on the left of the picture and the other on the right.

2 There is a rope between the two trees. It is about four feet from the ground.

3 Draw a man on the rope. He is walking from left to right. He is wearing a hat and he has a stick in his hand and . . . . ., etc.

They must decide how much detail they want to include (they can of course change their picture at this stage) but they must make sure that their instructions are clear.

The groups then exchange instructions and try to draw one another's pictures. As a final stage they check their pictures against the original ones.

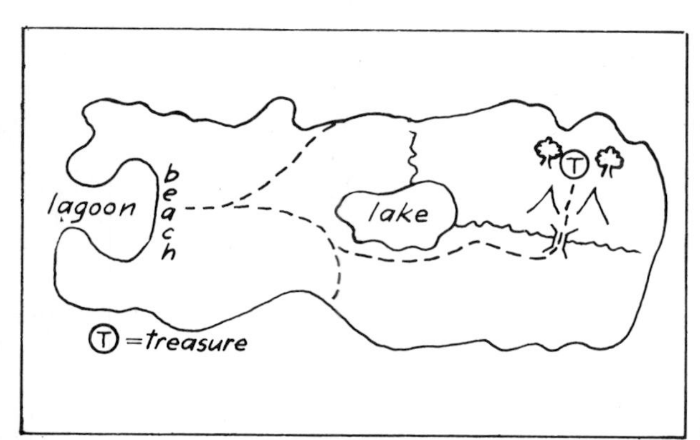

(j) *Headlines*

Give each group one or more headlines, like those shown on the next page. These can be invented or taken from real newspapers. Ask the students to discuss and write out the related story. At this level (and for the purpose of this activity) the students should not be asked to try to write a newspaper account of the story. The important thing is for them to use their *imagination*. Ideas are more important than formally correct language. If, however, the headline comes from a real newspaper, you can compare their version with the original. If all groups have the same headlines, you can also compare versions across the class.

Real or imaginary book titles can also be used to stimulate a similar activity. For example:

(k) *Graffiti*

Most students like to write on walls from time to time: this activity may encourage them to be more creative!

Give the students some examples of imaginative graffiti, like those below.

JOG – AND DIE HEALTHIER

Geography is everywhere

AVOID THE END OF THE YEAR RUSH – FAIL YOUR EXAMS NOW

Then ask them (individually, in pairs or groups) to try their hand at writing their own graffiti. It sometimes helps to suggest an event or a location.

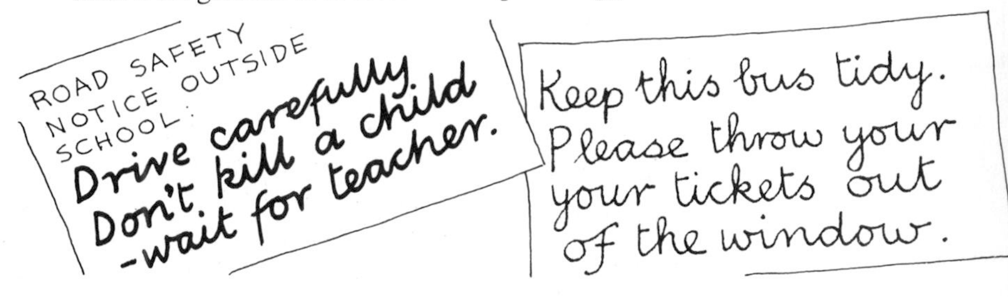


**Discussion**

1 Say whether you agree or disagree with the suggestion that:
(a) dialogue writing should be continued;
(b) some formal letter writing should be introduced.
Give reasons.

2 In what ways do many of the writing tasks proposed in this chapter involve a much closer integration than at earlier stages with other language activities in the classroom? Do you agree with this development?
3 Many of the activities proposed in this chapter would involve more class time being spent on writing. Do you think that this would necessarily be a wrong way of using class time? Give reasons.
4 Many of the activities in 5.5 and 5.6 are likely to result in the students making mistakes. Does this worry you?

**Exercises**

1 Devise other exercises similar to those in 5.2.1 for practising dialogue writing at the post-elementary level.
2 Devise an exercise similar to the one in 5.2.2 so that the cues are phased out and the students are asked to write the final text unaided.
3 Write an exercise, similar to the final one in 5.3 (d). After you have jumbled up the items, give the exercise to a friend for checking.
4 This is the complete text for 5.3 (a):

Janet West's sister is an air hostess for a famous international airline and Janet wants to become one too. However, she is still too young: the minimum age for an air hostess is twenty and Janet is only just over sixteen.

For the moment she has taken a job in an office. But she also attends evening classes. In particular, she wants to improve her French and Spanish because foreign languages are an important qualification for an air hostess.

Meanwhile Janet is gaining experience through her present job. For the office she works in is a travel agency. In this way she is learning not only how to deal with people but also quite a lot about the places she one day hopes to visit.

Now complete the exercise at the end of 5.3 (a) to practise grammatical and lexical cohesion.

5 Devise a rewriting activity, based on the text in 4 above, similar to one in 5.3 (c).
6 From your own experience of teaching (or learning) a foreign language, suggest other activities similar to those proposed for 5.5 and 5.6.

**References**

1 On guided writing see A Pincas (1982a) pages 102–9 and S Holden (ed) (1983) pages 49–57.
2 For the technique of interviewing the class see N Coe in S Holden (ed) (1983). Also L Winer on conducting a lesson through writing.
3 For written communicative activities see J Harmer (1983) pages 132–140.
4 For writing activities at this level see T Hedge (1983a and 1983b); T Jupp and J Milne (1980); A Pincas (1982b and 1982c) and L Woods (1986).
5 Examples of writing activities in this chapter have been taken from: D Byrne *Functional Comprehension* (Longman 1986 new ed.) 5.2.1(a); 5.2.2(b) and (c); 5.3(a)–(c) and (e); J Harmer *Meridian* (Longman 1985) 5.2.3(c); T Hedge *Pen to Paper* (Nelson 1983) 5.3(d) first example; M Palmer and D Byrne *Track 3* (Longman 1983) 5.6(b), (g) and (i) and A Pincas *Writing in English 1* (Macmillan 1982) 5.3(d) second example.

4) What was the result?
5) What was narrowly avoided?

This type of activity is a useful first step in getting students to make notes which they will do something with. It does not, of course, show them *how* to make notes, which is a problem we will now look at.

## 6.3 Note-taking and summarising

The relevance of the skills of note-taking and summarising* to writing tasks at this level should now be apparent: they are a common feature of many writing activities which relate in some way to what we have read or heard, since we often make a note of certain ideas and then re-present them in some other form. These, then, are important skills for the learners and it is essential that they should not be left with the impression that they are artificial 'classroom' activities, which are of little practical value except for the purpose of passing examinations, and this too only if they are executed according to certain formulas. This applies particularly to summarising. Yet this is how they are commonly presented and practised: the students are asked to take notes with no specific purpose in mind and to write summaries in a way which involves both distortion and contortion. It is not denied that there is an important element of control and discipline (or at least self-discipline) in these activities, but the purpose of this can best be brought home through meaningful activities rather than by procedures mechanically applied.

It should also be clear that these are skills that cannot be fully developed until the learners have reached a certain proficiency in the language, although it will be argued that we can and should first present them on a *receptive* basis. That is, the learners are *shown* what notes and summaries look like in relation to an original text. There are also *simple* tasks which the learners can be asked to perform before they carry out activities on a more extensive scale.

To appreciate just how difficult these skills are, even for the native user of the language, we would do well to consider what is involved in them. With note-taking, for example, we have to be able to identify key items in a text, which is in itself a searching test of comprehension and clearly much more difficult if we are listening rather than reading, when at least we have the opportunity to scrutinise the text at leisure. We also have to be able to reduce or compress these items in a way that is at least sufficient to allow us to retrieve their original meaning. The task of meaningful abbreviation calls for a good knowledge of how the language works. Likewise the ability to re-present these key ideas in such a way that they constitute an acceptable text, with appropriate sentence-linking and sequencing, is much closer to advanced than guided writing. While it may be true that, when we are summarising, the text provides us with the 'content' of what we write, in many respects it is more difficult to operate within the constraints of someone else's thoughts than to produce our own.

*For convenience, note-taking is used to refer to the activity both of *making* notes on a text which has been read and of *taking* notes on a text which has been heard. It is acknowledged that note-taking is itself a *form* of summarising. However, summarising is used here to refer to the activity of *re-presenting* a shorter version of the original text, although not according to any set prescription, such as using a given number of words.

### 6.3.1 Note-taking

It has been suggested that the initial phase of note-taking* should consist mainly of *showing* the learners what notes *look like* and of demonstrating that, although there are no magic formulas, since note-taking is to some extent a personal activity, there are a number of ways of reducing a text to notes so that the fundamental ideas in it are not lost. We should start, therefore, by *showing how notes relate to a text*. For example, we can present both a text and a set of notes and examine how the writer arrived at his notes.

> John Smith, who was born on December 6,1951, is a secondary school teacher. His wife's name is Joyce. They have three children: one son and two daughters.

> J Smith born 1951/ teacher/married, with 3 children

We may also usefully contrast one set of notes with another. For example:

> John Smith Born : 6.12.51 Sec. school teacher
> Wife : Joyce 1 son 2 daughters

By comparing two *possible* sets of notes we can ask the students to identify what information has been preserved in both and what other information each writer has included or omitted. We can also examine some of the devices which have been used. For example, the examination of even short sets of notes like these reveals that we can omit pronouns, auxiliary verbs, articles and connectives, and that we can also use numerals and symbols. We can also begin to look at the question of abbreviations, of which there is only one example in the notes (*sec.* for *secondary*) and discuss how this was made (i.e. in this case, by taking the first syllable of the word) and whether other ones are possible (for example, *sch.* for *school*).

It will also help students to be shown different ways of setting notes out. For example, the model below does not commit them to any particular order, and, perhaps more important, allows additional related information to be added in at the right point, especially if you are reading a long text. For example, where John Smith was born, the name of the school he teaches in and the subjects, etc.

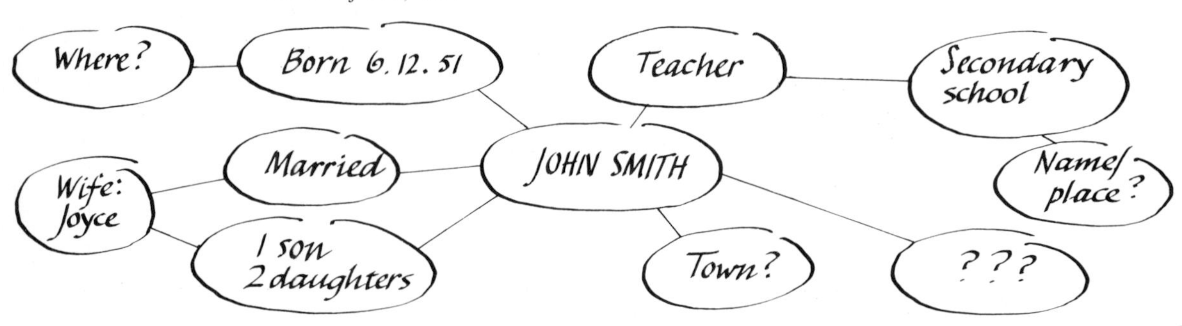


*This can be begun at an earlier stage and practised from time to time as a preparation for more extensive note-taking activities.

In addition to asking the students to examine sets of notes along these lines, we may take a number of texts and discuss how we might arrive at a set of notes: for example, we can underline key items, bracket words or phrases that can be omitted, and consider possible contractions. Finally, we can *work out with the students* a possible set of notes.

Another useful activity, to be carried out with fairly long texts, is to ask the students to identify the main ideas in a text. For example, as a first step, we can give them a list of the main ideas, presented in random order, and ask them to put these in the order in which they are dealt with in the text. Subsequently, they may be asked to identify the main ideas for themselves.

At this stage, too, when we first ask the students to take notes, it is helpful, both in order to focus their attention on specific aspects of the text and to ensure that they keep their notes short, to give them some sort of framework within which to work, in the form of a chart to be completed. The activities on page 75 show how it is possible to focus the attention of the students on particular aspects of a text (in this case, one for reading followed by a related one for listening to), which are the points they need to make a note of. Students enjoy this kind of activity because it is intrinsically more enjoyable than simply making a string of notes. Equally important, however, the use of charts obliges students to be concise.

Many games and gamelike activities involve keeping notes, and this is another way of bringing home to the students their real importance. One activity in particular will be found useful: this is a variation on *Describe and draw*.

Instead of trying to draw a picture which someone describes for them without their being able to see it, the students make notes as they listen. They can then compare notes and subsequently, either individually or in collaboration, carry out one of the following tasks:

— describe the picture orally;
— draw the picture;
— write a description of the picture

Usually the students feel more comfortable making notes as a first stage (rather than being asked to try to draw the picture straight off) and, of course, the activity does give them an immediate use for the notes they have made.

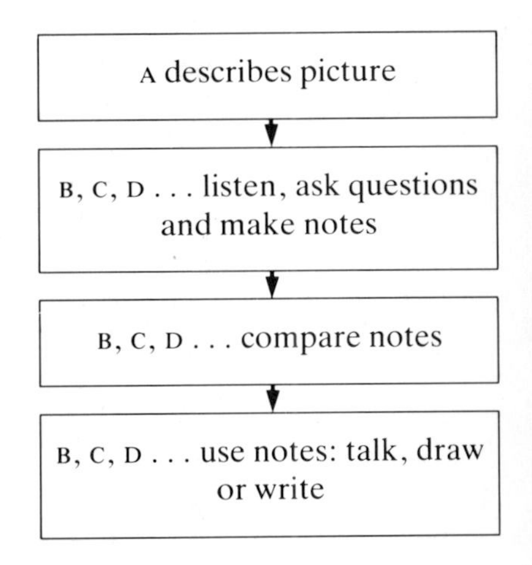

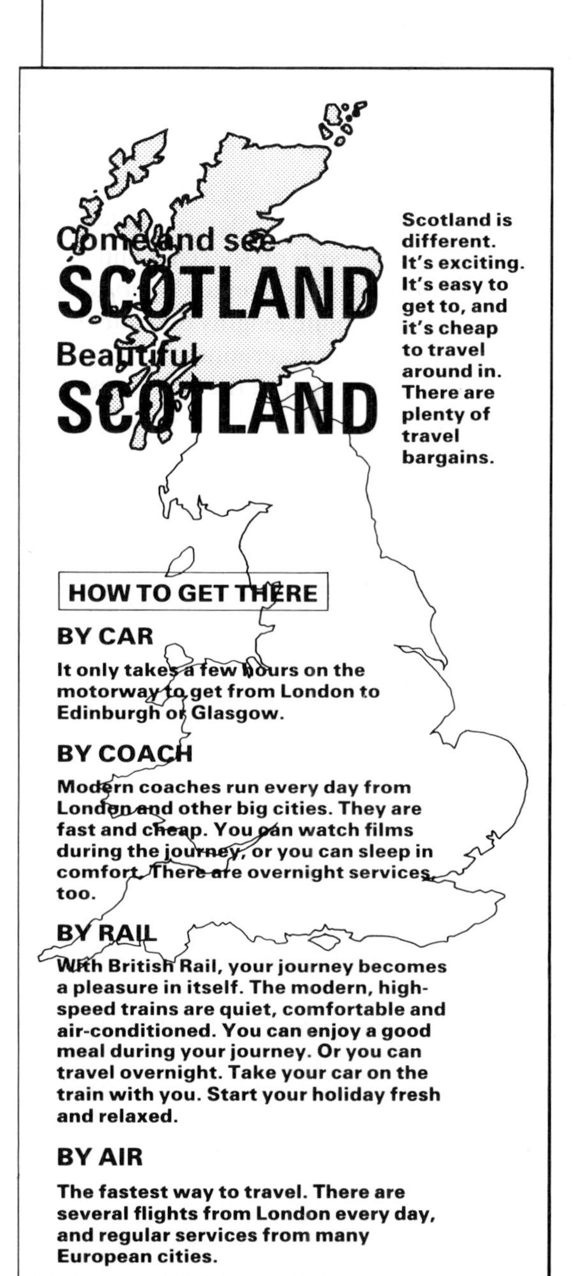


**1 Use information in the text to complete this table. If there is no information, put a question mark.**

| | coach | plane | train |
|---|---|---|---|
| daily | | | |
| overnight | | | |
| with meals | | | |

**2 How would you travel if you wanted to do these things?**

a) watch a film on the journey
b) take your car to Scotland without driving it
c) get to Scotland as quickly as possible

**3 Listen and answer:**
Mr Smith wants to go to Scotland, so he goes to a travel agency. The travel agent tells him different ways of travelling. How does Mr Smith decide to go to Scotland? Why?

**4 Mr Smith wants to know how long it takes to get to Scotland. What does the travel agent tell him? Listen to the conversation again and complete this table:**

| | How long? |
|---|---|
| train | |
| plane | |
| coach | |

**5 Complete this table:**

| WAYS OF TRAVELLING TO SCOTLAND (for one person) | |
|---|---|
| quickest | |
| cheapest | |
| most comfortable | |

Through activities along these lines (and also within the broader context of simulations, see 8.4), the skill of summarising may be practised and developed *in a realistic way*. The requirements of examinations may demand that this skill should be used in a much more limited way, such as making summaries in the traditional sense, for which the *purpose* may not be at all apparent, but these need not be allowed to distort the way we teach and practise this skill in the classroom.

**Discussion**

1 Make a list of the things you use note-taking and summarising for. Arrange these under two headings: *frequent* and *occasional*. Compare your list with a friend.
2 From your reading of 6.3.2, do you agree that summary writing is an important and valuable activity?
3 How effective do you think the final activity in 6.3.2 would be for teaching summary writing?

**Exercises**

1 Examine any textbook at an appropriate level to see what attempt is made to practise note-taking and summary writing. Are the activities well presented?
2 Do the exercise in 6.2.1.
3 Make notes on the text in 6.2.1, using the diagram model shown in 6.3.1. Do you think it is more suitable for this type of text than conventional forms of note-taking?
4 Find a suitable picture and try out the *Describe and note* in 6.3.1 with some friends. What difficulties did you have?

**References**

1 The text on page 71 comes from R O'Neill: *Flight* (Longman 1973).
2 On note-taking see JB Heaton in S Holden (ed) (1977) *Keep it short* and JB Heaton (1975) pages 18–28.
3 On summarising see M Donley (1975).
4 The illustrative material on page 75 comes from M Palmer and D Byrne *Track 3* (1983).

# 7

# Contexts for writing: the use of visual material

## 7.1 Some general considerations

At first glance, visual material offers an attractive and stimulating framework for writing practice, especially if some form of picture sequence is used, and for this reason no doubt the learners generally respond favourably to tasks which relate to some kind of visual context. On the other hand, if we consider the kind of writing activity which often results from the use of visual material — narrative and descriptive 'composition' with no specific goal in mind, except that narrative tasks could be said to take the form of telling a story — it is clear that visual material can easily lend itself to the practice of writing for writing's sake, of a kind that has no communicative value and which will not contribute significantly to the development of writing skills. Part of the problem at least seems to be the *level* at which visual material is generally used: for the most part, this is at a fairly early stage of the course, when 'picture composition' writing in particular tends to be accorded a special place in the programme. As we have seen, visual material *can* be appropriately used in the early stages, to supplement other forms of practice, but what needs particular consideration is its use at a more advanced level, where the learners need guidance rather than control and where the contexts it offers can be more fully exploited. The main concern of this chapter will be to identify the kinds of writing activity which can be derived from different types of visual material at the post-elementary level.

### 7.1.1 Types of visual material

We may divide visual material into two main categories:

(a) *Pictorial*: this category includes *single pictures* and *picture sequences*.
(b) *Plans, maps, diagrams*: diagrams include material such as graphs and charts (i.e. they contain *figures* and perhaps a few items, such as headings, in *words*).

### 7.1.2 The use and abuse of visual material

By its very nature visual material provides a much more open-ended framework for language practice than texts. The visual content does of course determine *to some extent* the language which can be used, particularly in the lexical area, although even here we are not tied to any set of items. In other respects, however, we are free to exploit the material as we wish. *The special advantage of this is that we can use the same piece of material at different levels and also for different types of writing.*

On the other hand, the very fact that visual material is open-ended has its dangers. There is the risk that the learners will interpret the visual content in a more sophisticated way than their proficiency in the language permits. This may involve some form of mental translation, which in turn results in inappropriate and incorrect expression. Even if errors are not our main concern, it is undesirable that they should result from the learners failing to make full and proper use of the language they have acquired: both oral and written practice must, as one of its goals, aim to show the learners how they can express themselves within the limits of the language they know. Writing tasks, therefore, have to be very carefully defined and the learners given appropriate preparation for them.

If visual material is used at too elementary a level, it also tends to encourage a form of written expression which is remote from writing in any real sense. At best, it might be described as a kind of commentary on what can be seen in the picture. Thus, for example, the learners are invited to produce sequences using the Present Continuous. For example: *John is at the bus stop. He is waiting for the bus. The bus is coming and John is going to get on it. Now he is getting on the bus*, etc. Although it might be argued that the learners will get more satisfaction from writing sequences of this kind rather than producing single sentences, this type of writing will not benefit composition skills. On the contrary, it might even to some extent be harmful because it allows the learners to *believe* that they can write without the use of appropriate linking and sequencing devices. It is, surely, much better to use alternative forms of practice (as suggested in Chapter 4) rather than to encourage them to write in a way which is inappropriate to the written form of the language.

## 7.2 The role of the teacher

Visual material clearly has great potential as an aid to developing writing skills and can provide both contexts and stimulation for a variety of activities but, unless it is properly used, it may create more problems than it solves. It is essential, therefore, to do the following:

(a) *Identify and define an appropriate writing task which relates to the theme of the visual material.*

The students may of course be given a choice or be asked to work on different but perhaps complementary activities. It is unlikely that the writing task will call for any form of straight narration or description, which is an aspect which may be explored through oral preparation for writing. On the contrary, the writing task should have a clearly defined form (a letter, a report, etc.), which will deal with the theme from a particular angle or viewpoint.

(b) *Identify the language which the learners will need in order to carry out the task.*

As far as possible, language difficulties should be anticipated at the oral preparation stage and further explored, if necessary, through supplementary exercises. In order to do this, it will generally be necessary actually to write out a version of the writing task to see what language it entails.

(c) *Decide how to prepare the learners for the writing task.*

The classroom preparation stage is a delicate one. As was noted in (b) above, we want to ensure that the learners have the necessary language for the task they are set. At the same time, the writing activity must never be simply a replica of the oral preparation, otherwise there is no challenge in the activity. If the writing task involves dealing with the theme presented from a different angle or viewpoint, the problem is largely resolved, because the learners have to decide how to restructure and select from the language practised at the oral preparation stage.

## 7.3 The use of visual material: some examples

This section contains some examples of how visual material may be exploited at the post-elementary level for different kinds of writing task.

### 7.3.1 Using a map to practise paragraph construction

The following activity is based on a simple map like the one shown below, which may be drawn on the board or reproduced on a transparency for use on

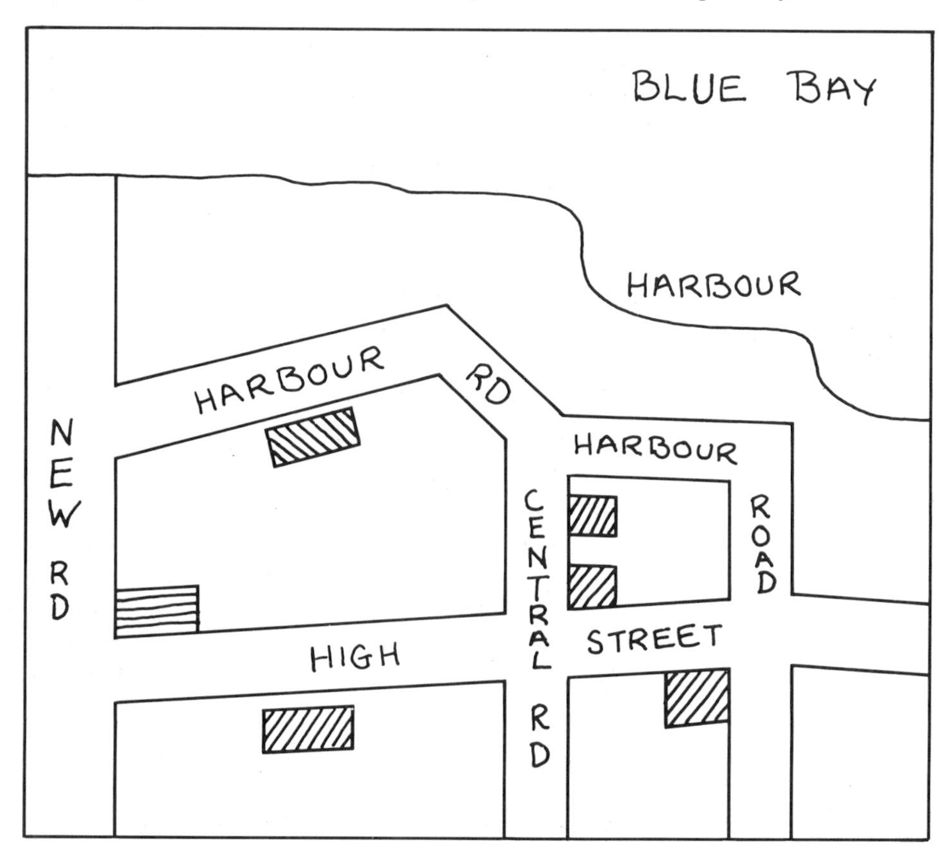

the overhead projector. It has been found effective in getting the students to explore ways in which a paragraph can be organised. In particular, they have to consider both the necessary and possible sequencing of certain sentences and different ways of linking these sentences.

Each student, or pair of students, if they are asked to work together, is given a card which contains a piece of information about three of the places shown on the map. Two examples of such cards are given below.

*The building in Harbour Road between Central Road and New Road is the market.*

---

*The library was built in 1935.*

---

*Fred Cash is also the owner of the Palace Cinema.*

*In one part of the Palace Cinema they show all the latest films.*

---

*The market is open from 8 a.m. to 2 p.m. on weekdays.*

---

*The supermarket sells all kinds of food, except fish.*

The information written on the cards is obtained by breaking down a paragraph describing each of these places. For example, the description of the market runs as follows:

> The building in Harbour Road between Central Road and New Road is the market, which was built in 1875. It sells fish, vegetables and fruit. It used to sell meat, but that is now sold in the supermarket. The market is open from 8 a.m. to 2 p.m. on Tuesdays, Thursdays and Fridays, and from 8 a.m. to 5 p.m. on Saturdays.

The information which appears on ten different cards is as follows:

1. The building in Harbour Road between Central Road and New Road is the market.
2. The market was built in 1875.
3. The market sells fish.
4. The market sells vegetables.
5. The market sells fruit.
6. The market used to sell meat.
7. Meat is now sold in the supermarket.
8. The market is open on Tuesdays, Thursdays, Fridays and Saturdays.
9. The market is open from 8 a.m. to 2 p.m. on weekdays.
10. The market is open from 8 a.m. until 5 p.m. on Saturdays.

The students are then invited to identify a building which the teacher points to, such as the market. Only one student is able to do this and he therefore informs the rest of the class. This statement is clearly the opening sentence of the paragraph. Another piece of information which might relate to this is then called for. Since the students do not know what is on one another's cards, several suggestions are likely to be made until it is agreed that the most suitable piece of information is: *The market was built in 1875*. However, it cannot follow on from the first sentence in the form in which it appears on the card and suggestions are invited as to how it should be linked to the preceding sentence. This may be either with *which*, as in the original version, or with *it* (that is to say: *The building . . . is the market. It was built in 1875*). It should be noted that most of the statements on the cards *have* to be modified in some way.

And so the construction of the paragraph continues. Notice that we are not concerned to reconstruct the original text in its *exact* form. On the contrary, it is far more important to get the students to consider acceptable alternatives. For example, the text might continue: *The market sells fish. It also sells fruit and vegetables* or even: *The market sells not only fish but also fruit and vegetables*.

The completed description of the first place may be written up on the board. After that, the students can be asked to make notes while the activity is in progress and to write up the descriptions afterwards. They will find this easier to do if they are working in pairs.

### 7.3.2 Visual sequences for the production of dialogues

Visual sequences of the kind depicted on page 84, where the dialogue is implicit in the situations, have to be interpreted rather than described. There are two main ways in which the dialogue element may be 'extracted':

(a) The students may be first asked to say what they think the pictures are about. For example, in Picture A, the woman, whom we will call Mrs Ball, wants some sugar. (*Why does she need it?*) She asks her husband to go and get it. (*What words does she use?*) Perhaps at the start her husband is reluctant to go. (*Why? What is he doing?*) So she has to persuade him. (*What does she say?*) The students are then invited to suggest various possibilities for each line of dialogue.

(b) Alternatively, the dialogue may be cued by providing the first line of the exchange. In the example below, which relates to Pictures A and B, the teacher takes the part of Mrs Ball, and the students give her husband's responses.

T: Will you go to the grocer's and get some sugar, please?
S: (But I'm watching a football match on TV.)
T: Well, if you don't go, I can't make a cake.
S: (Oh, in that case, I'll go!)
T: Now, I need some other things as well . . . salt, coffee . . . Here's a list.
S: (I don't need a list!)

The students may be asked to suggest *several* alternatives for both speakers. For example:

MRS B: I need some sugar. Can you go and get me some?
MR B: Now? I was just reading the paper.

Or:

MRS B: Would you mind going to the grocer's for me?
MR B: What do you want?
MRS B: Well, I've run out of sugar . . .
MR B: I'll go this afternoon. I've got to go into town.
MRS B: Yes, but . . .



Thus, when the students come to write up their dialogues, they can select from the different suggestions that have been given or produce similar ones for themselves.

The next three pictures may be similarly exploited to produce, for example, a short conversation about gardening and the weather (C), Mr Ball ordering the things he wants from the grocer — but forgetting the sugar (D) and a conversation about the news (E). Picture F involves asking for and giving directions and is therefore an important picture which should be exploited in depth (see below). Finally, in G and H, we have the conversation between Mrs Ball, who is angry because her husband has taken such a long time, and her husband, who tries to make excuses — only to find that he has forgotten the sugar!

For Picture F, it is suggested that one or more model dialogues should first be built up with the help of the class, to practise language relevant to asking for and giving directions. For example, we might start with a very simple dialogue:

MAN: Excuse me. Can you tell me the way to the station?
MR B: Yes. Cross over the road, go as far as the newsagent's and then turn left.
MAN: Is it a long way?
JACK: Oh, about half a mile.

The purpose of producing these dialogues, it should be emphasised, is to rehearse the *language* which the students will need for their writing task. When they come to write up their dialogues, they should be encouraged to produce very different versions.

The dialogues written about individual pictures in the sequence may be further elaborated to form a short play, divided into scenes and with appropriate 'stage directions'. This is best done as group work. The example below shows that this can be done in fairly simple language:

*Scene 1 Mrs Ball is cooking in the kitchen. She finds that she does not have any sugar.*

MRS B (*calling her husband*): Jack!
*There is no answer.*
MRS B: JACK!
MR B (*coming into the kitchen*): Yes. What is it?
MRS B: Oh! I've run out of sugar. Could you go to the shop and get me some?
MR B: But I wanted to . . . (etc.)

### 7.3.3 Other uses for visual sequences

Whatever the final outcome in writing, you can use visual sequences like the one in 7.3.2 and the shorter one below for a range of oral activities both to prepare for written work and to involve the students in the material (which we must never assume to be *intrinsically* motivating, however attractive it may appear to be). For example:

— *speculation*: Get the students to give their own ideas about the people and the setting (who they are; where they are, etc.). See 4.6 (i).
— *roleplay and dramatisation*: Get the students to work out how they would present people shown in the pictures and how they would act out some or all of the sequence. (See below for related writing activities.)
— *discussion*: Most picture sets will stimulate some kind of discussion. For example, husband-wife relationships for 7.3.2 and monsters for the set below.

Some key writing activities will be:

— *notes*: The students should make a note of any important ideas which come up during oral work.
— *diary entries*: The students write up an account of what happened from the viewpoint of one of the people in the sequence. Notice that this involves selective reporting. For the sequence above, don't forget the diary of the monster!
— *role descriptions*: The students write rolecards for one another if they are going to act out the sequence. See 4.6 (f) and 5.6 (d). They can also write scenarios (see 5.6 (e)).
— *letter writing*: Similar to the previous activity. Again the activity will involve selective reporting — and, if you do not wish to bore the person you are writing to — realistic summarising!

— *reports (articles, etc.)*: This will depend on the content of the sequence. The students could write one for the one above. For example: THE MONSTER THAT CAME TO LUNCH! Report writing is discussed in detail in 7.3.5.

None of this precludes more basic oral work (question and answer, true-false statements, etc.) and more basic written work (sentence linking, paragraph completion), which may be necessary with certain classes.

### 7.3.4 Techniques for presenting visual sequences

Much will depend on the form in which this is available (book, display chart, transparency), and also how much you want the students themselves to contribute ideas. Wherever possible, unless you want to give them the task of exact description (which can be a challenging activity if it is presented in the right way), you should welcome the opportunity of getting the students to contribute ideas. They are certainly likely to enjoy it more than if they are allowed to describe only what they can see.

Here are some ways of presenting a four-picture sequence so as to stimulate the students' imaginations:

(a) *Show the first and last picture. The students fill in what happened in between.*

| A | ? | ? | D |
|---|---|---|---|

(b) *Show the middle two pictures. The students supply the beginning and the end.*

| ? | B | C | ? |
|---|---|---|---|

(c) *Show the last picture only. The students decide what happened before.*

| ? | ? | ? | D |
|---|---|---|---|

(d) *Show the first picture only. The students decide what happened after that.*

| A | ? | ? | ? |
|---|---|---|---|

If for any reason you cannot use incomplete sequences, you can ask the students to *continue* the story.

For the use of jumbled sequences, see 7.3.8 (h).

### 7.3.5 Using visual material for report writing

The picture on page 88 could of course be used for a variety of writing activities. It could be exploited for the production of dialogues, such as one between the two cyclists or between the lorry-driver and the motor-cyclist if an accident is narrowly averted, or for letter-writing. For example, *any* of those involved in the incident might write a letter about it at some subsequent date. Report writing has been chosen to demonstrate that, if visual material is used at the post-elementary level, it has great potential for formal writing tasks.

A single picture has been chosen for this purpose to show that, properly exploited, it can be just as effective in providing a context for this type of writing activity as picture sequences. In fact, there is even some advantage in using a single picture, because it is more open-ended: the outcome, an accident or a near accident, is not actually *shown* and we can therefore decide for ourselves what form it might take.

On the assumption that an accident *did* take place, we might set as a writing task a newspaper report of some kind. Other possibilities are reports made by the lorry-driver (for example, in connection with an insurance claim) or by a policeman investigating the accident. For this, the events we can actually see in the picture — a lorry approaching a sharp bend in the road, two cyclists talking as they overtake the lorry and two men on a motor-cycle, whose attention is distracted by a plane that is landing, coming in the opposite direction — are likely to be referred to in some way in the report but not necessarily in their chronological order. At the oral preparation stage, therefore, we can get the students to describe these events without any risk of prejudicing the writing task.

Our classroom presentation should also aim to arouse the interest of the students in the theme and at the same time to help them with some of the language they will need in the report. We might begin, for example, without necessarily referring to the picture at all, by discussing some of the things that cause accidents. These can be listed on the board:

Causes of accidents

— fast driving
— careless driving (for example: . . . .
— mechanical defects
— weather conditions
— pedestrians

Examples of the language used to describe road accidents can be given or elicited.

Features of accidents

— vehicles collide/get damaged/run people over/knock people down
— people get killed/injured/taken to hospital, etc.

We can then relate these items to what is shown in the picture and decide which ones apply, or might apply depending on the outcome of these events. It is at this point that we can get the class to decide, after considering several suggestions, what actually happened.

If the students need further help with writing reports of this kind, then we can work out on the board with them *one* account of the accident and ask them to use different facts in their version. For example, we might begin by deciding on a suitable headline and showing that this is followed by an important piece of information.

CYCLIST KILLED ON AIRPORT ROAD

One cyclist was killed and another badly injured when they collided with a motor cycle on the road to Winton Airport yesterday afternoon.

We can then show that at this point we would probably use information provided by the picture. For example:

> . . . The collision occurred near a sharp bend in the road about two miles from the airport. According to the driver of the lorry, which was travelling towards the airport at the time, the two cyclists . . .

In the version which the students are asked to write, the outcome of the picture might be that the driver of the lorry hits the tree, and is killed or badly injured, through trying to avoid the motor-cyclists. This will still allow the students to use some of the language of the rehearsed version, but at the same time they will have to make quite significant changes. In this way, none of the challenge of the writing activity is lost.

### 7.3.6 Using diagrammatic materials

We have already seen how maps can be used for controlled and guided writing (see 4.3(b) and 5.3(d)), while earlier in this chapter (7.3.1) a map was used to guide paragraph organisation. The same material can be used at a later stage for freer writing activities, such as writing a letter to advise someone how to get to your house or where to meet you in town. These, together with graphs like the one below (see Exercises, page 94) plans of rooms and buildings and bus and train timetables can be used for a variety of activities which will encourage students to write *precisely*. For example, there may be more than one way of describing a room or advising a route — but at least it will be clear if the students have got the information across.

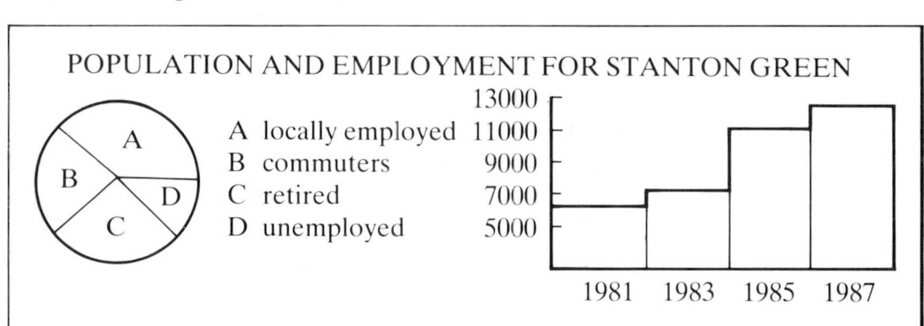


Much of the language which the students will need for certain formal types of writing, such as reports, will involve in particular the use of functions typical of the written language, such as defining, comparing and contrasting, exemplifying (etc.). The practice of these (see 9.2) can help to give a new slant to the programme and enable us to cover old ground in a new way. Visual material in the form of plans and diagrams can be very useful for this purpose.

The example below shows how the diagrammatic representation of a town can be used to introduce some of the language needed for writing a text which involves the systematic classification of data and also to structure a parallel writing task for the students to carry out.*

The diagram below shows the structure of a town called Brunton.

INDUSTRIAL ESTATE
Industries
1 4
2 5
3

RESIDENTIAL AREA
HOUSING ESTATE PARK
Types of Building Facilities
1 1
2 2

COMMERCIAL SECTOR
Shops/Offices
N

With the help of the diagram we can elicit from the students the three main areas into which the town is divided and where they lie in relation to one another. This may be done by asking questions. For example: *How many parts does the town fall into? What are they? Where are they?* With the help of this information we can give a general description of Brunton in our opening paragraph. Some key language is indicated in italics.

Brunton *falls into* three main parts: the industrial *estate*, the residential *area*, and the commercial *sector*. The residential area *lies between* the industrial estate *on the north side* of the town and the commercial sector *on the south*.

As a next step, we might show the students how one part of the town may be systematically described. For example, the residential area. This is partly structured through the diagram, but the students are also invited to make some suggestions for themselves. Again using appropriate questions, we can build up a description as follows:

The residential area *consists* of a housing estate and a park. *The former* is made up of two main *types* of buildings: detached houses and blocks of flats. *The latter* has some excellent facilities. These *include* a football ground, a swimming pool, a tennis court and a children's playground.

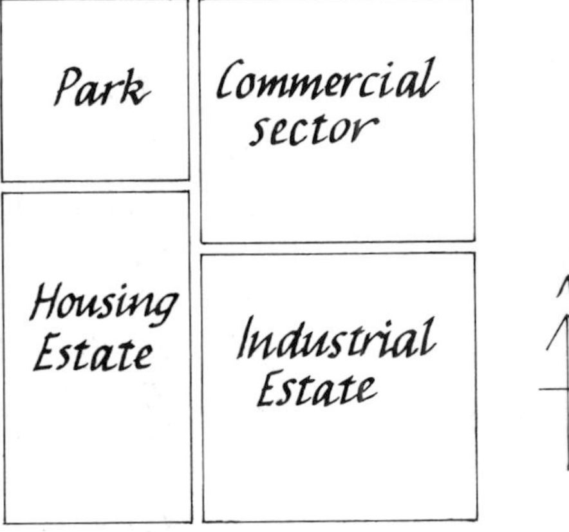


*This does not cover all the language needed for writing texts where the main function is one of classification. Some items can be more effectively presented and practised through textual models. For a more complete unit, see 9.2.1.

The students now have the key language needed to describe the two remaining parts of the town along the same lines. Again they can contribute to the text by suggesting, for example, the main types of industries, shops and offices to be found in these two areas.

For their parallel writing task, the students are given a diagram of a town with a different structure as shown in the second diagram on page 90.

The students may also be given an outline for the beginning of their report, together with a reminder of the key language items which may be used, along the following lines:

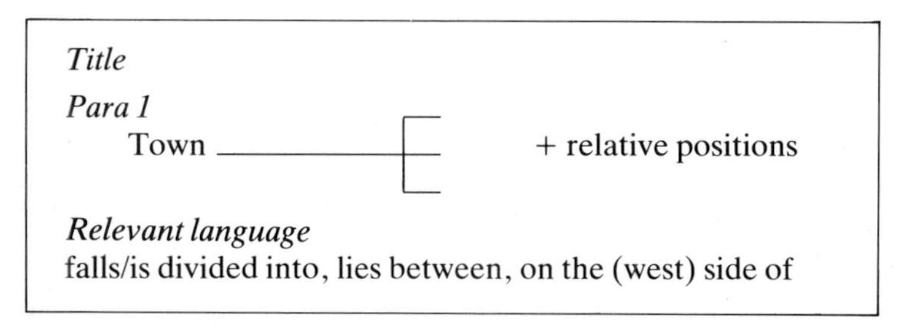


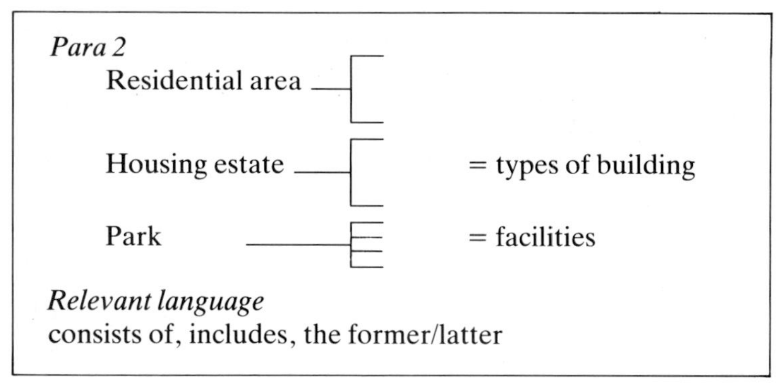


### 7.3.7 Other useful visual materials for writing activities

(a) *Ads*: These must occupy a special place for a number of reasons:
- there is a wide variety of them;
- they are widely (and freely) available;
- students respond to them.

If you are collecting or making ads, cover key areas such as jobs, accommodation, things for sale, holidays, language schools, food, cars and clothes — but also include in your collection any ads that are particularly striking and memorable.

Writing activities will normally involve some roleplay such as writing for more information (e.g. in connection with holiday accommodation) making an application (e.g. for a job or for a place in a school); writing letters of complaint (e.g. about food ads), etc.

(b) *Programmes*: For example, for cinemas, theatres, festivals, TV and radio (see 4.6 (d), where the students made their own). These can be used for planning activities which involve making notes or writing short reports, or for writing letters (e.g. suggesting the programme for a day out).

(c) *Menus*: These are mainly useful for oral interaction but can be used to stimulate a writing activity, such as describing a very good meal you have had, which has a natural built-in sequence.

### 7.3.8 Writing for fun

Visual material has been used for a number of 'fun' writing activities in earlier chapters. See, for example, 4.6 (d) TV/radio programmes; 4.6 (f) rolecard pictures; 4.6 (i) pictures for interpretation and speculation (an activity which is especially valuable as students make progress with their writing); 5.6 (h) jigsaw writing and 5.5 (i) instructions for drawing a picture or a map.

Some other activities are suggested below. The first three involve the use of small picture cuecards (usually showing a single object such as a piece of furniture, an item of clothing, an animal, etc.).

(a) *Picture linking*

The students, working in groups, are given (or are allowed to choose from a larger number) three to four pictures, around which they have to make up a story. The objects should not have any obvious connection, so the students are encouraged to be imaginative — and even absurd!

(b) *Lost and found*

Each student is given two cards (e.g. a dog and a pair of shoes) and uses one of these to write a notice about something he has lost and the other to write a notice about something he has found. The cards are then redistributed and the notices read out. The students respond by saying 'That's mine!' or 'I've got it!'

FOUND (in my garden)
One pair of very old

LOST One small white dog.
Its name is Maggie.
WARNING It barks a lot
and bites!

(c) *Desert Island messages*

After the students have played the Desert Island game (that is, when they imagine they are marooned on an island and have to decide how they will use (3) objects such as a hammer, clock, mirror), they can be asked to write messages to put into a bottle and throw into the sea. They can also be asked to write their diary for part of the time they are on the island.

TO THE PERSON WHO FINDS THIS!
Please tell my family I
am safe, well – and
happy! I don't want
to be res

(d) *How much can you remember?*

Each group of students is given a picture, which they look at for about a minute. They then turn the picture over and, working individually, write down as many things as they can remember about the picture. They then use these notes to work together to build up a complete description of the picture (orally or in writing), which they compare with the actual picture.

(e) *Who is it?*

Each group is given a picture of a famous person (or place) and has to write a precise description of it. The descriptions are then passed round the other groups, who try to identify the people (or places).

(f) *Life story*

Each group is given a picture of a face (not anyone known) and has to make up the life story of the person (e.g. who (he) is; what (he) does for a living; things that have happened to (him)). The students should of course aim to be as imaginative as possible.

(g) *Cartoons*

The students work in pairs or groups to write captions or speech bubbles for cartoons or other suitable pictures.

(h) *Jigsaw stories*

Give each group a cut up picture composition sequence (see 7.3.4), so that each student or pair of students in the group has one picture. Each student or pair then writes down what their picture shows. The students then put away their pictures and use their notes to try to work out what the complete sequence is about by exchanging information.

(i) *Ads*

Give each group of students a picture showing, for example, a car or a hotel and ask them to write an exaggerated advertisement for it.

(j) *Postcards*

Give each student a postcard (made by pasting a picture cut from a magazine or travel brochure onto a piece of card) and ask them to send a message to someone else in the class (this may include you!). They may do this as themselves or in the role of a famous person (e.g. singer, actor, politician . . .).

**Discussion**

1 What are some of the advantages and disadvantages of using visual material as a framework for writing practice?
2 Do you agree that, on the whole, it is better to use visual material at the post-elementary level? Give reasons.

**Exercises**

1 Most 'picture composition' material available in published form is intended for use at a fairly elementary level. Examine any set of material of your own choosing and see whether it could be successfully exploited at a more advanced level.
2 With reference to the activity described in 7.3.1, write a description, similar to the one of the market, of another place (for example, the supermarket or the Palace Cinema) and then divide up the text into statements which can be sited on the students' cards (as shown on page 82).

3 Identify some writing tasks which could be set on the following picture composition sequence. These should be in the form of dialogues, letters or reports. Suggest the kind of preparation that might be needed for any one of these tasks.

4 Select any piece of visual material and show how it could be used for a report writing activity along the lines suggested in 7.3.5.
5 Suggest some uses for the graph in 7.3.6.
6 Work with a friend and try out one or more of the activities in 7.3.8. Can you suggest other activities along these lines?

**References**

1 For examples of visual material for writing activities, see JB Heaton (1966); D Byrne (1967); JB Heaton (1975); C Fleming (1975); R Ridout (1975); D Byrne (1976); LA Hill (1978); L Markstein and D Grunbaum (1981); JB Heaton (1986); D Byrne (1988).
2 Other composition books that contain useful visual material are: T Hedge (1983a, 1983b and 1985); R Knight (1986); A Pincas (1982b and 1982c) L Woods (1986).
3 For techniques for exploiting picture composition material imaginatively see D Byrne (1987) *Picture Composition: A Fresh Look*.
4 The picture in 7.3.5 is from JB Heaton *Beginning Composition through Pictures* (Longman 1975); the picture sequence in 7.3.3 is from M Palmer and D Byrne *Track 3* (Longman 1983) and in Exercise 3 from G Fleming *Guided Composition* (Hodder and Stoughton 1975).

# 8

# Integrated skills

## 8.1 The importance of integrating skills

The need to integrate skills in language learning has already been stressed and in many respects this is not a new feature of the writing programme. In fact, many of the communication activities and 'fun' writing activities in Chapters 4 and 5 integrated talking and writing (and sometimes reading) in a natural way. See, for example, questionnaires and quizzes in 4.6 (a) and (b); roleplay activities in 5.5.1; scenario writing in 5.6 (e); jumbled stories in 5.6 (g) and writing instructions for pictures and maps in 5.6 (i). The key factor with many activities is *how* you get the students to work: pair and group work offer many more opportunities for integrating skills, as the simple analysis below shows. The activity is drawing a picture or a map.

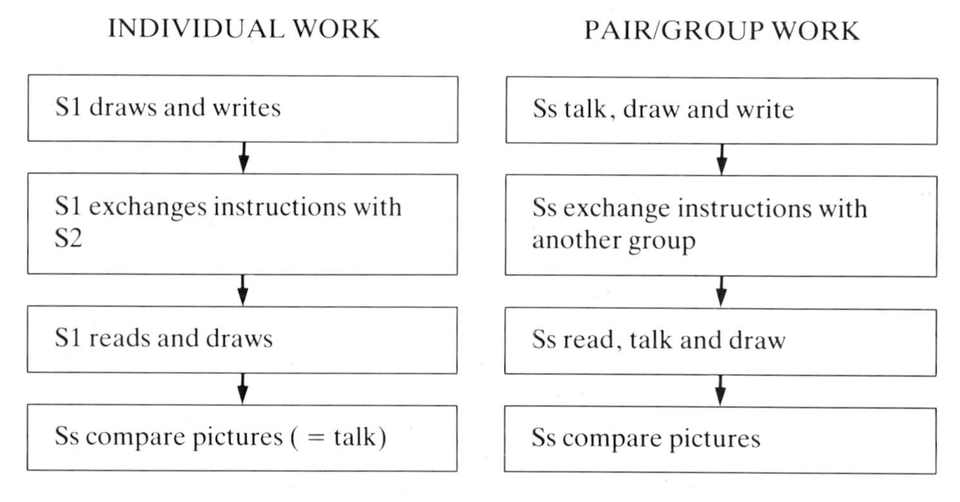


If, therefore, you want to increase the amount of skill integration in your daily teaching — and this is worthwhile because it allows the learners to *use* language naturally, not just *practise* it (notice how in many of the activities language is used to *get something done*) — make sure you use pair and group work for reading and writing activities.

For many classes this may be enough. At the intermediate level, however, you will probably want to increase the amount of fluency work you do with your students and three ways in which you can do this through integrated skills activities are discussed below.

## 8.2 Project work

Project work cannot be neatly defined because it takes so many forms. It usually involves some research (through interviewing and reading); it often involves going out of the classroom (although this is not essential) and it almost always involves discussion.

The *process* — carrying out the project — is clearly important because of the activities the students have to undertake; but equally the *product* — some kind of document — will give them a great deal of satisfaction. Writing may take place at both stages: along the way (filling in questionnaires, making notes) and at the final stage when writing up the project. (For our purpose we would avoid one that resulted, for example, in drawing plans or maps, though this could be a legitimate project in itself.)

In the language classroom it is important that project work should give the students opportunities for language use and development. At the same time it will help them on a broader educational front to develop:

— communication skills: when interviewing and reporting back;

— research skills: when reading;

— social skills: when discussing, collaborating.

Sometimes for project work the students will have to use the mother tongue (e.g. when talking and reading), but the outcome in writing will always be in English.

### 8.2.1 Organising a project

Although this is largely a matter of common sense (since there are no 'rules' for something that does not have a set form), projects have to be carefully planned and sustained. The teacher's role is crucial especially in presenting the project and involving the students in it, and in ensuring that it does not break down. You may like to follow these stages:

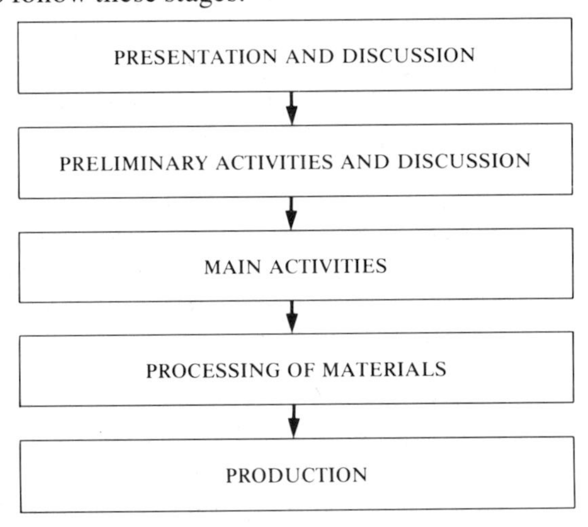

One of the things you may have to do with the students at the start is to show the students how to 'open up' a topic. One way is to get them to make a chart similar to the one used for note-taking in 6.3.1, which will involve talking and writing. For example, if the topic for the project is Food, a chart might look like this:

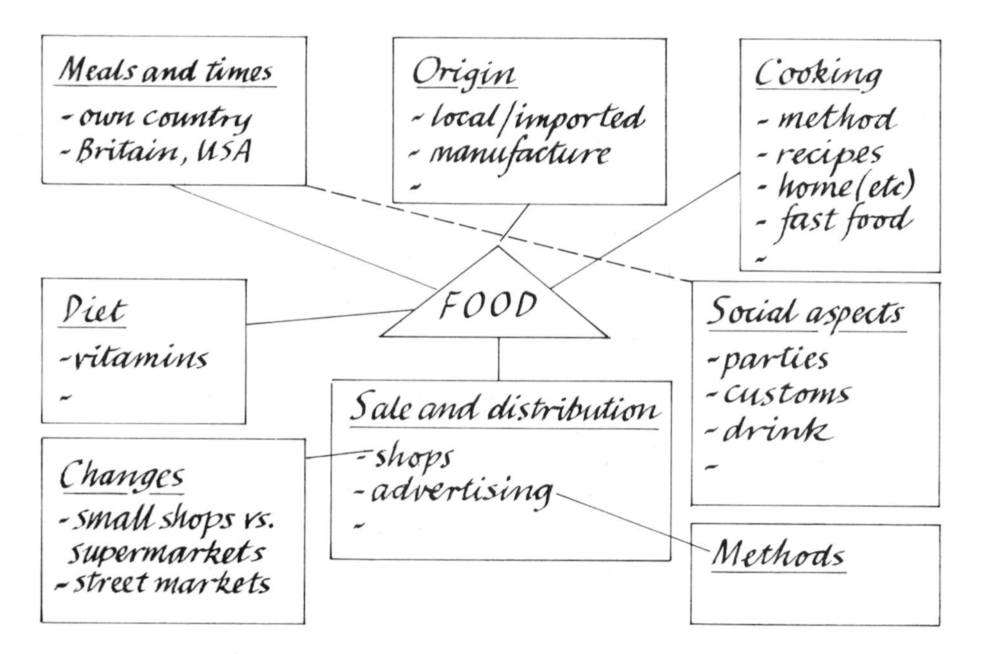


At the presentation stage, it should be enough to establish some main aspects and then divide the students into groups to discuss and develop them. The groups may work on all aspects simultaneously or on one particular aspect only. In either case note-taking will be involved (perhaps together with some initial reading). At this point the scope of the project should be agreed: for example, it could be decided to limit or extend its scope. This may depend on research opportunities (opportunities for going out of the classroom, available reading material, etc.) or simply the interests of the students.

When this has been agreed and the work distributed among the groups, the students can begin work on the main activities. If this involves interviewing, (for example, about eating habits, attitudes, social behaviour), questionnaires will have to be devised, and this involves precise writing. If these involve reading (as some certainly will, whether in English or the mother tongue), the students must be prepared to summarise and re-present what they have read, perhaps also translating from the mother tongue into English.

At some point the groups will have to report back on their research to date and also to agree what their final product will look like. It is assumed that this will be a brochure or booklet of some kind, consisting of text and illustration, which will be attractive enough for someone to want to read (e.g. students from another class). The students will then have to do a good deal of writing up and editing of their material. If they are asked to work within the constraints of a certain length (sixteen pages), they will probably have to do a certain amount of summarising. They will have to do some thinking about the actual presentation of their material, so that the end-product does look attractive. All this — apart from providing a framework for integrating skills — will make writing a motivating activity.

Your involvement throughout will be important but mainly as a consultant, as for other forms of group activity. The students should be encouraged to ask for your advice (for example, where they can find relevant reference material. In some class situations you may actually have to provide it) and for your help with their English (depending on their level and the extent to which you want them to rely on themselves). The responsibility for the final product must of course be their own.

### 8.2.2 Suggestions for projects

The suggestions for projects below have been roughly grouped under headings but inevitably they overlap.

(a) *'Newsmag'*

This is a long term project, perhaps extending over the whole of the school year, which involves researching (e.g. visits to newspaper offices, reading about the history of newspapers and magazines) and writing material for a hybrid product — a combination of a class newspaper and magazine. Items to be included are articles, creative writing, reviews, fun features (crosswords, puzzles, jokes), ads, special topic areas (e.g. sport) and illustrations. Even if you omit the outside visits, which would be primarily of educational interest unless you have access to English medium newspapers, the advantage of this project in the English language classroom is that it has something to offer everyone in the class.

(b) *Projects that could be done mainly through reading (in and out of class) and sharing of knowledge*

Food, analysed in the previous section, could be done mainly in this way. Some other topics are:

- time
- money
- transport
- uses of materials (e.g. plastic, paper, etc.)
- clothes

(c) *Projects that could be done mainly through interviewing family and friends*

- eating habits
- leisure (perhaps subdivided into sport and hobbies)
- TV viewing habits
- shopping habits

(d) *Projects involving real or imaginary planning*

- developing facilities in one's town (see 5.5.2 (a))
- developing an imaginary island
- planning an imaginary trip to the moon, down the Amazon, across the Sahara, etc.

— planning an ideal town, shopping centre, house, school, club, recreation ground, etc.

## 8.3 Skill sequences

In real life we do not use language skills in any set order — certainly not in the order that they often appear in textbooks: listen → speak → read → write. We use skills as and when we require them. For example, we see an ad in the paper (for a job or a holiday); we may talk about it to someone or ring up or write a letter about it. (We may of course simply forget about it!) This 'chain' of activities could go on — and on! Importantly, however, it can provide a model for integrating skills in a realistic way at a post-elementary level and, incidentally, provide natural contexts for writing. Once the mechanism for this is understood, it is not difficult to set up a chain of activities in this way.

### 8.3.1 Oral work leading to guided writing

In this example, a conversation provides the setting for a note-taking task, which the students perform simultaneously with the 'characters'. They are then shown how these notes were used to write a notice, which was the reason why the notes were made, and are subsequently asked to write a second notice themselves. Thus all four skills are practised in a *fully* integrated way.

1 *Bill Halliday and Jane Stokes, his girlfriend, are planning to go on holiday together. They want to travel round Britain together because Bill, who is an Australian, has not seen much of the country. They are in Jane's flat and they are talking about their plans.*

JANE: . . . Well, I don't want to go by train. But why don't we hire a car?
BILL: Hm, it's very expensive, you know. And *you* can't drive! . . . But you've given me an idea! Perhaps we could get a van.
JANE: You mean *buy* one?
BILL: Yes, a secondhand one. One of those big ones.
JANE: But, Bill, they cost a lot . . . and besides, there are only two of us.
BILL: Look, we only need about six people. You, me, and four more. We can share expenses. It's a marvellous way to see the country — camping, staying in hostels . . .
JANE: Mm, but how do we *find* four people? Put an ad in the paper?
BILL: No, too expensive. Listen, I'll put a notice up on the board at college. There's one near the bookshop.* And what about that newsagent's near the record shop? They have ads in the window.
JANE: OK, then. Well, I suppose we ought to make some notes . . . .

1A *Bill and Jane continue to talk.** Jane makes notes. Listen, and make a note of the important points.*

JANE: Right, here's some paper . . . and a pen. I'll make the notes.
BILL: OK. Well, first . . . must be able to drive. After all, *you* can't and I don't want to drive all the time!
JANE: . . . has to be able to drive. And we want people who like a simple life. After all, we're going to camp and stay in hostels.
BILL: Yes, definitely no luxuries! Have you got that down?

*Bill works in a college bookshop and Jane works in a record shop.
**The students hear the conversation which follows.

JANE: Hang on! Yes, and another thing . . . they ought to share the cooking too. I'm not going to do it all!
BILL: Should be able to cook, then. Right. What else?
JANE: Shall we tell them about the cost of the trip?
BILL: Mm, yes. Let's say . . . about £25 each. Plus expenses.
JANE: . . . £25 and share all expenses. What about age?
BILL: Good point. How about . . . eighteen to twenty-five? And not all English!
JANE: Or Australian! So . . . eighteen to twenty-five . . . any nationality. That should encourage people.
BILL: . . . Do you think that's all?
JANE: Can't think of anything else. We've got quite a few notes.
BILL: OK, then. I'll write out the notice for the board at college.
JANE: . . . And I'll do the one for the newsagent's . . .

2 *This is the notice which Bill put up on the college noticeboard the following day.*

2A *Now write the notice which Jane Stokes took to the newsagent's. Her telephone number at the record shop is 874 9192 and her number at home is 675 3245.*

YOU! YOU! YOU! AND YOU!
ARE YOU BETWEEN 18 AND 25?
CAN YOU DRIVE?
CAN YOU COOK?

I AM TRYING TO ORGANISE
A FOUR WEEK TRIP ROUND
BRITAIN IN A VAN

PLACES FOR FOUR MORE PEOPLE
* ANY NATIONALITY WELCOME!
* NO LUXURIES!
* SHARE ALL EXPENSES!
* SMALL CHARGE: £25 each
CONTACT: Bill Halliday
College Bookshop

### 8.3.2 Reading leading to free writing

In this example, the sequence opens with a reading activity. It includes guided as well as free speaking and writing tasks. It should be noted that, at the end of the sequence, the students *themselves* decide what happens.

1A *Terry Barnes, a teenager**, *is getting tired of his job at Holford Natural Products, so he decides to look for a new one. He sees these ads in* The Holford News.

Personnel Manager, HNP, Holford.

LAB. ASST. 16-21. Prev. exp. desirable. Gd. prospects for right person. Trafalgar Tobacco Co. Holford 7997 Ext. 5.

JUNIOR ACCOUNTS CLERK to work for Eastern Bus Co. 5 day wk. 9-5.30. Prev. exp. not essential. Typing an advantage. Apply in writing.

SHORTHAND TYPIST

*The students have background information about Terry from another part of the story.

1B *Terry first rings up the Trafalgar Tobacco Company. Listen to his conversation with the secretary.*

SECRETARY: Extension 5 . . . Mr Platt's secretary. Who's speaking, please?
TERRY: Oh, my name's Barnes. I'm ringing about that vacancy you advertised in The Holford News . . .
SECRETARY: Which one was that, now? Was it for a lab assistant?
TERRY: Yes, that's right . . .
SECRETARY: Well, I'm afraid we've already filled that vacancy. I'm very sorry.
TERRY: Oh, well, thanks very much. Goodbye.
SECRETARY: Goodbye.

1C *Terry next rings up the Eastern Bus Company. He is told by the secretary that the job is still available, but that he must apply in writing. Suggest what they actually said to each other.*

2A *Complete this letter which Terry writes to the Eastern Bus Company.*

July 10

Dear Sir,

I am writing to apply for the job of Junior Accounts Clerk, which was advertised in The Holford News.

Now say:
- how old you are
- where you are working
- what job you do
- whether you have had any previous experience of accounts
- whether you can type

My former class teacher at Holford Comprehensive, Mr T Newman, will send you a reference if you require one.

Yours faithfully,
T. Barnes
T. Barnes.

2B *This is the letter which Terry got from Mr Davis, the manager of the Eastern Bus Company.*

July 16

Dear Mr Barnes,

Thank you for your letter of July 10. I should like you to come for an interview on Friday July 23 at 10.30. Could you please telephone my secretary and confirm this.

Yours sincerely,
S. Davis
S. Davis.

2C *Terry phones Mr Davis' secretary. He explains why he is ringing and confirms that he can come. Suggest what Terry and the secretary said to each other.*

3A *Terry is being interviewed by Mr Davis. Suggest what Terry said.*

MR DAVIS: Right, Terry. Sit down. Tell me something about yourself.
TERRY: ..................
MR DAVIS: And how long have you been in your present job?
TERRY: ..................
MR DAVIS: Oh! I'm surprised you want to leave, then.
TERRY: ..................
MR DAVIS: Well, I've had a word with Tom Newman. But I'd like to speak to your present employers. Is that all right?
TERRY: ..................
MR DAVIS: Well, thanks very much for coming along. We'll let you know sometime next week.
TERRY: ..................

3B *Mr Davis finally decides to offer Terry the job. This is the letter he wrote.*

July 30

Dear Terry,

I am pleased to be able to offer you the job of Junior Accounts Clerk at a starting salary of £100 a week. Would you please confirm that this is acceptable. Can you also let us know when you would be free to start?

Yours sincerely,
S. Davis
Sam Davis.

3C *Write Terry's reply, accepting or declining the job.*

4A *The following week, Terry meets Carol Davis, a girl he was at school with. She is the daughter of Sam Davis. Terry tells Carol what he has been doing recently. Suggest what he said.*

4B *Afterwards, Terry realises that he 'quite likes' Carol. He decides to write to her. Write the letter which he sends her.*

4C *Write Carol's reply.*

## 8.4 Simulations as a framework for writing activities

Many of the writing activities proposed and discussed so far have involved an element of roleplay. That is to say, the students are asked to assume the parts of different characters. (See, for example, 5.5.1 and 8.3). The use of simulations enables us to take this kind of work a stage further both by providing a framework for integrated language work in which the learners themselves provide a larger 'input' of the data from which the writing activities are derived and by allowing them, where this is appropriate to the situation, to *be themselves* within a defined setting. This latter feature has an obvious advantage when we are working with groups of learners who share certain professional skills and interests and who are learning a foreign language with these primarily in view, since motivation will be increased through the utilisation of their specialist knowledge. With non-specialist groups, however, whether adults or adolescents, we shall probably have to continue to rely largely on roleplay, although we may be able to introduce a certain amount of role simulation, where the learners react to the task as themselves. For example, in the simulation described in 8.4.2 below, some students in a secondary school class can play the part of teenagers, while others will be asked to take on adult roles. For our present purpose, what is more important is the extent to which the activities which they are asked to carry out generate meaningful and relevant opportunities for writing. At this level, simulations would seem to be ideal, providing *guidance*, in the form of a well-defined setting, which gets as near to real life as we can hope to in the classroom, as well as *motivation* for executing the writing tasks.

### 8.4.1 Devising a simulation

While care must be taken with the construction of a simulation, especially if we want to ensure that it leads naturally to certain writing tasks, this need not be viewed as a complex task. By definition, the simulation will involve the discussion of a specific problem or set of problems, and the context within which this takes place must be clearly defined for the learners. To do this in a natural way and, no less important, to activate all the language skills, we must provide the learners with an adequate amount of background information.

Thus, in the simulation described in 8.4.2, the *problem* to be discussed relates to the Holford Arts Centre, which has been criticised for failing to provide the public with the right kind of cultural programme. In addition, to add an element of spicy interest to the situation, the Centre is also accused of allowing certain 'undesirable happenings' to take place on the premises. The *setting* is a public meeting, at which invited speakers as well as members of the public discuss these problems. It is left to the participants, through what they say within the limits of their roles, to decide on these issues. Thus the speakers themselves provide the raw substance for the writing activities.

To establish the setting, there is a certain amount of *background information*, devised by the teacher, which consists of material both to be listened to and read. The other component contrived by the teacher is the specification of the roles of the participants. This is done through *role cards*, which either define or suggest, depending on the role to be played, the line to be followed by each participant. We may also, either on the role cards or through a preliminary oral briefing, help the learners with certain *items of language* which they can use in the discussion.

The simulation described in 8.4.2 is perhaps a little different from most

TEACHING WRITING SKILLS

## *Reporters*

L BARON
As a reporter for *The Holford News*, your main task is to write an account of the meeting for next week's edition. Make sure that you include the main points. You would also like to make your report slightly sensational, although this is likely to bring you into conflict with your editor.

P BLAKE
Your task, as secretary to the meeting, is to write a concise but accurate report on the meeting, to serve as a record for future reference. If you are not sure of any point made at the meeting, you can check it with the speaker concerned afterwards.

J STOTT
At the meeting it is likely that teenagers will be criticised. In the light of what is said by various members of the public you must decide what action to take. For example, you may want to write a letter to the editor of *The Holford News*. Alternatively, or in addition to writing the letter, you may decide to start a public protest on behalf of youth freedom. For this purpose, you will have to write a notice for public display, and perhaps some slogans.

W TRAILL
Your main task is to report the meeting for Holford Comprehensive School magazine. In your account, you should focus in particular on matters which concern teenagers. You are also very ambitious, and you would like to be a reporter when you leave school. You hope that the account you write will catch the attention of the editor of *The Holford News*, to whom a copy of the school magazine is sent.

T SMITH
As a member of Holford Amateur Dramatic Society and a close friend of G S Potterton, you are determined that the views of the Society will get a wider hearing after the meeting. Your main task is to write either a letter to the editor of *The Holford News* or a circular letter to be sent to members of the public. In your letter make appropriate references to what was said at the meeting.

J WISEMAN
As a reporter for *East Anglia Radio*, your main task is to produce a short account of the meeting which will appeal to listeners of *East Anglia at One*, a lively lunch-time programme of news and views. In this connection, you may also wish to interview, for example, the Director of the Centre *after* the meeting.

T JENKS
As a reporter for *The Cambridge Gazette*, your main task is to write an account of the meeting for next week's edition. Make sure that you include the main points. Personally, you would like to see an Arts Centre, similar to the one in Holford, in Cambridge and you should therefore draw attention to its achievements and play down or ignore some of the criticisms of the Centre.

### 8.4.3 Exploiting the simulation for writing tasks

The main purpose in describing the construction of this simulation in detail and in particular showing the 'input' required from the teacher was to demonstrate that it provides a powerful framework for a variety of writing tasks. For example, before the meeting, those who have been invited to speak will want to make some notes on what they propose to say. At this stage, to ensure the involvement of the whole class, it is suggested that the reporters should look at various kinds of writing relevant to their tasks. For example, news reports, letters to the editor, notices, etc.

While the simulation is actually taking place, everyone is fully occupied, either in speaking or in listening and taking notes. After the simulation, the reporters are engaged in writing up their various accounts.

At the same time, however, we have to provide writing activities for those who spoke at the meeting. Clearly this will depend to some extent on the actual outcome of the meeting, which is by no means predictable, but, as a general guide, activities along these lines are suggested:

(a) The chairman of the meeting may be asked to work with the secretary on the task of editing and writing up the formal account of the meeting.

(b) The Director of the Arts Centre (depending on the outcome of the meeting) may either write his letter of resignation or work out a new style programme of activities for the Centre. This may be done in collaboration with, for example, one adult and one teenage member of the public and with one of the students from the Polytechnic.

(c) The Youth Welfare Officer, together with the Principal of Holford Comprehensive and two or three members of the public, including teenagers, may be asked to draw up a proposal to improve the facilities of the Youth Club.

(d) The Secretary of Holford Amateur Dramatic Society may work with his representative at the meeting on the letter to *The Holford News* or on the circular letter, depending on which task is taken up.

(e) One student from the Polytechnic, together with two or more members of the public, may draw up *their* proposal for a revised Arts Centre programme, to be submitted to the Director for consideration.

(f) Other members of the public, adults and teenagers, may be asked to write either letters to the press or 'anonymous' letters to various people, such as the Director of the Arts Centre or the Secretary of the Amateur Dramatic Society, making accusations against them.

It should be clear that there is no difficulty in devising interesting writing tasks for *everyone* in the class. All of these tasks derive quite naturally from the simulation. The result of this is that we end up with a considerable body of material, produced by the students themselves, which can be read aloud or circulated round the class and which is of real interest to everyone.

**Discussion**

1 Do you agree with the importance attached to skill integration at this level? If you disagree, can you suggest other ways of ensuring that writing activities are purposeful?
2 Examine any textbook of your own choosing to see what attempt is made to integrate skills at this level. Consider in particular whether writing follows on

naturally from the other activities, especially oral work, or whether it tends to be presented as a homework task.

3 Can you see any problems arising from the suggestions for project work in 8.2? Do you think the advantages outweigh these?
4 Do you think the simulation outlined in 8.4 provides sufficient guidance for the writing activities involved? If you wanted to give the students more guidance, how would you do it?
5 Which of the different types of activity suggested for integrating skills do you find most attractive? Why?

**Exercises**

1 Examine any textbook to see what provision is made for project work. Could some of the activities suggested be developed into small projects?
2 Draw a chart similar to the one on page 97 for any of the topics suggested in 8.2.2 (a).
3 Show how you would present and develop for classwork any of the suggestions in 8.2.2 (a).
4 Analyse the sequence of activities in 8.3.2, following this model. This will help you to understand the underlying mechanism.

| TEXT | OUTLINE OF CONTENT | SKILL |
|---|---|---|
| Ad | TB reads ad in Holford News | Reading |
| Dialogue | TB rings up Trafalgar Tobacco Co | Listening |

Now construct a similar sequence of your own. This may be much shorter than the one in 8.3.2.

5 Write role descriptions for other speakers in the simulation in 8.4.
6 Suggest some alternative roles for the 'reporters' in the simulation in 8.4, together with related writing activities.

**References**

1 On integrated skills see D Byrne (1986) Ch. 11 and A Matthews et al (eds.) (1985) pages 32–4 and 126–40.
2 For project work see D Byrne (1986) pages 133–7. This section also contains more information about 'Newsmag'. Suggestions for developing an imaginary island are given in A Matthews et al (1985) pages 126–31. A useful book on project work generally is D Waters (1982), from which the chart for Food on page 97 has been adapted.
3 For skill sequencing see D Byrne in K Johnson and K Morrow (1981). The first sequence in 8.3.1 is based on D Byrne and S Holden *Going Places* (1980); the second sequence on D Byrne and S Holden *Insight* (Longman 1976). For material based on this model see D Byrne and S Holden *Follow It Through* (Longman 1978) and *Going Places* (Longman 1980). Also R White *Write Away* (Nelson Filmscan 1987).
4 On simulations see K Jones (1982). For a simple introduction see D Byrne (1986) pages 125–8. The simulation in 8.4 is based on D Byrne and S Holden *Insight* (1976). Comparison with the original material will show how textbook material can be adapted for this purpose.

# 9

# Writing at the post-intermediate level

## 9.1 Problem areas

It is often assumed that, once the learners have acquired a reasonable proficiency in written expression, further practice in this skill can be given mainly through tasks in the form of some kind of 'composition' or 'essay'. The students are given a topic or a theme and are expected to express themselves at some length on it in order to demonstrate their ability to write. It might seem that, having avoided this type of activity at earlier stages of the programme, we are obliged to fall back on it at this level in order to give the learners *extensive practice* in their hard won skill.

Since compositions and essays are still a feature of many public examinations, clearly we should not deny the students some preparation for this type of task. This aspect is considered in 9.3. We must also attempt to see what skills are practised through this kind of writing and whether the same skills can be more effectively practised in alternative ways. At the same time, it would be wrong to accept this kind of writing activity as one of the main outcomes of the writing programme. For one thing, it is a form of writing which is rarely practised outside the classroom or examination hall. One needs only to ask: when did I last write an essay? Besides, for most of us, it presents an extremely difficult task, even in our mother tongue, and even more so if we are asked to do it against the clock. There would seem little point, therefore, in inflicting this type of writing activity on the foreign language learner, whose proficiency in writing is unlikely to match the task.

It was noted above that we would need to consider alternative ways of developing skills practised through composition and essay writing. These we may assume to be particularly those skills involving the ability to organise ideas in a sustained piece of writing. But organisational skills, which certainly need further practice at this level, can be equally well developed through activities which involve some realistic form of expression, such as letter and report writing. Reacting to a situation through writing, for example, a letter of protest, will require argument, while the marshalling of relevant facts to support this argument will involve organisational skills. Unlike composition writing in the traditional sense, however, the learners can be more fully involved in this type of writing task, through some kind of roleplay, and can appreciate its relevance to real life. In terms of developing writing skills, therefore, the learners' needs can be fully met through further practice in letter and report writing.

Composition and essay writing also provide opportunities for what is often called 'free expression': the learners are allowed to say what they like on a given topic or theme. While it is true that at this level control of what the learners write (except for remedial purposes, see 9.2) would be inappropriate, we still have the responsibility for providing them with an *adequate context* for writing activities. Ideally, this kind of framework should be provided through activities such as the simulation described in 8.4, which have the further advantage of fully integrating all the language skills. In practice, because of the shortage of class time, we may have to be satisfied with much less. It is stressed, however, that writing tasks should not, simply for the sake of convenience, be divorced from other classroom activities which involve listening, speaking and reading. The link with reading is the most easily established, and of course commonly practised at this level, if only in the form of asking the students to write about something they have read, but the close association of speaking and listening with writing is less common. Yet a class discussion, for example, can provide an excellent springboard for writing activities: ideas have been discussed, points of view expressed and, what is especially important, interest in the topic has been aroused. All this, especially if the learners have been asked to make notes during the class discussion, can lead on quite naturally to a variety of writing activities in the form of letters, reports, newspaper articles and so on. Similarly, project-type work, carried out in small groups over a period of time, provides excellent opportunities for skill integration. The learners have to discuss the content of the project and invariably have to do a considerable amount of reading for it, while the writing up of the project is in itself a purposeful activity.

The possibility of individualising writing practice was noted in 1.6. At this level, as the learners become increasingly aware of how writing may relate to their future needs (for example, for occupational purposes, for academic study or perhaps only for personal communication), motivation can be increased by paying particular attention to these. If, for example, a group of students in the class express a particular interest in learning commercial correspondence, because they feel that this is the type of writing which will be, or is most likely to be, of relevance to them, even the setting of fairly *formal* tasks becomes more acceptable. Needs for individualised writing practice can to a large extent be met through the use of self-instructional material, with the students working together in pairs or groups.

A final point to keep in mind is that, as we allow the learners increasingly more opportunities for self-expression through writing, we must view what they write as *attempts to communicate something*. We owe it to the students, of course, to correct and evaluate their work to the extent that this will *improve* their performance especially in examinations, since these are often weighted in favour of written skills, but it would be wrong to destroy both their interest and confidence in writing through excessive correction. One thing we can do is to separate tasks which are designed to improve their examination performance, and which therefore can be viewed more critically, from those intended to develop communication skills on a broader basis, such as the activities which formed part of the simulation in 8.4. For these in particular it is important that the teacher should not be the only consumer and, in the classroom situation, this means that the students should be writing *for one another*. This element of having *something to communicate to somebody* is naturally present in activities like simulations and projects: because there is a diversity of task, the students are genuinely interested in knowing what others in the class have written. And, because of their involvement in the activity, they are likely to be as critical of what has been written as we would ourselves. The difference, however, is that they react as *readers* rather than as *judges*.

### 9.1.1 The main features of the writing programme

(a) *Provision should be made for remedial work.*

It is suggested in 9.2 that one way of doing this is using a functional approach to writing skills. This component of the writing programme will also ensure that the learners are given further help with the problem of organising their written expression at the level of content.

(b) *Opportunities for free expression should be increased.*

This does not imply, however, that the learners should simply be set tasks for writing, in the form of topics or themes. It is suggested that a framework for writing activities should be established through the use of activities like those in Chapter 8.

(c) *Writing activities should be in the form of realistic tasks such as report and letter writing.*

Most of these formats for writing practice have been only superficially explored at previous stages and there are therefore opportunities for dealing with these in depth at the post-intermediate level, instead of resorting to some type of essay writing to give extended practice in writing. Proficiency in specific varieties of writing may also be developed to take individual needs into account. It should be kept in mind that this aspect of the writing programme must be supported by *exposure* to appropriate models through the reading programme.

(d) *Examination requirements should not be neglected.*

Other components of the programme will ensure that the learners continue to extend their range of writing skills but, to the extent that mastery of specific forms of writing, such as essays, is a feature of public examinations, these needs must be taken into account.

## 9.2 Remedial work: the value of a functional approach

It is inevitable that some remedial work will become necessary at this stage. While it is possible to select and repeat certain activities from earlier stages of the programme, the adoption of a functional approach to writing skills has certain advantages. In general, it can be used to give a new slant to the programme, so that familiar ground can be explored in a new way. The same is no less true of oral skills, where a similar need is likely to be felt. Thus, whereas at previous stages, reinforcement activities may have focused mainly on structural items, we can now, for the purpose of remedial work, review these items under the umbrella of particular language functions, such as expressing requests, suggestions, invitations, etc. It is not suggested that all this will be totally new to the learners; it is the *systematic* treatment of these functions, bringing together language which the students have already mastered, which is likely to be different. In particular, however, it will enable us to explore in greater depth other functions, which occur typically in longer stretches of language, such as comparing and contrasting, generalising, exemplifying, defining. See the Appendix, Section A for a comprehensive list of these. Mastery of these functions will be especially valuable in helping the students to organise their written expression.

An example of a unit of work, dealing with comparison and contrast, is given in 9.2.1. While it is not suggested that the content is suitable for all types of learners, the procedures are likely to be of general validity. Thus, the students are first exposed to a text which exemplifies the various items of language needed to express comparison and contrast. Their attention is drawn to the key items, which include some alternative forms, although it is not suggested that the students are being given any more than a 'basic kit'. As a second stage, they are given opportunities for using these items orally, so that they can explore their use in a fairly flexible way. At this stage, certain difficulties show up which were not perhaps anticipated through the reading text. Finally, the students are given an appropriate writing task, which shows how the function of comparison and contrast relates to a specific communicative purpose.

### 9.2.1 Expressing comparison and contrast: a specimen unit

(a) *Study the language of comparison and contrast in the report below*:

| KEY LANGUAGE | REPORT ON EXHEAD AND PORTSEA |
|---|---|
| *in many ways*/in some respects/to some extent, *alike*/similar, *both, each, like, similarly*/likewise/in the same way, *but, dissimilar*/different/unlike, *compared with*/in comparison with, *while, on the other hand, unlike, difference between, however*/in constrast/on the contrary | Exhead and Portsea are two towns on the south coast which are *in many ways* very much *alike*. They are *both* old towns and *each* has a large harbour.<br>*Like* Portsea, Exhead has a population of approximately 120,000. It also has a growing number of local industries. *Similarly*, Portsea is expanding on the industrial front, too.<br>*But* in other respects the two towns are quite *dissimilar*. For one thing, *compared with* Portsea, Exhead is a much more attractive place. For this reason it is a popular holiday resort in summer, *while* Portsea, *on the other hand*, attracts very few visitors.<br>*Unlike* Portsea, Exhead has extended its hotel facilities because of the tourist trade. One striking *difference between* the two towns is that Exhead has located its new industries on an estate outside the town. In Portsea, *however*, there are even factories near the harbour. |

(b) For the next stage, the students are given a bio-data cue-sheet and work in pairs, contrasting and comparing any two of the people described. For example, they make statements like: *In many ways, J H Smith and A P Wheeler are very much alike. They were both born in 1939, they are both married*, etc. Or: *Compared with Michael Webb, Andrew Wheeler is a rich man!*

Notice that, at this stage, the students have to *identify* the points of comparison and contrast, as well as *use* the appropriate language.

1

| | |
|---|---|
| Name | John Henry Smith |
| Date of Birth | December 6 1939 |
| Marital status | Married<br>2 children (1 son, 1 daughter) |
| Occupation | Teacher |
| Income | £10,400 p.a. |
| Car | Ford Sierra (1983 model) |
| Sports | tennis, golf |
| Other interests | travelling, theatre, photography, chess, stamp collecting |

2

| | |
|---|---|
| Name | Michael Webb |
| Date of birth | December 12 1955 |
| Marital status | Single |
| Occupation | Teacher |
| Income | £7000 p.a. |
| Car | Fiat Strada (1986 model) |
| Sports | None |
| Other interests | dancing, travelling |

3

| | |
|---|---|
| Name | Andrew Peter Wheeler |
| Date of birth | April 1 1939 |
| Marital status | Married<br>5 children (4 sons, 1 daughter) |
| Occupation | Architect |
| Income | £18900 |
| Car | Ford Sierra (1986 model) |
| Sports | golf |
| Other interests | photography |

(c) For their final task, the students are given data in tabular form. They are asked to write a report on one of the cars in each of the two groups, recommending this car as the 'best buy'. They have to compare and contrast this car with other ones in the same group, where this is appropriate.

| | FIAT Panda 750 | VAUXHALL Nova | RENAULT TL | FORD Fiesta 950 |
|---|---|---|---|---|
| Price (£) | 3390 | 4186 | 4805 | 4201 |
| Cubic capacity ($cm^3$) | 769 | 993 | 1108 | 957 |
| Length (ft., in) | 11 1 | 13 0 | 11 9 | 12 0 |
| No. of seats | 4 | 4 | 4 | 4 |
| M.p.g. | 45 | 37 | 48 | 40 |
| Max. speed m.p.h. | 78 | 89 | 89 | 85 |

| | BMW 316 | CITROEN CX 20 | ROVER 216SE | VOLVO 240GL |
|---|---|---|---|---|
| Price (£) | 7795 | 9149 | 7509 | 8960 |
| Cubic capacity ($cm^3$) | 1766 | 1995 | 1598 | 2316 |
| Length (ft., in.) | 14 2 | 15 3 | 13 8 | 15 8 |
| No. of seats | 4 | 5 | 4 | 4 |
| M.p.g. | 26 | 23 | 32 | 21 |
| Max. speed m.p.h. | 108 | 110 | 102 | 110 |

## 9.3 Free writing: some suggested procedures

The main concern of this last section is to suggest some procedures which students can use when they have to cope with the task, which very few of us find easy, of producing a text in the form of a 'composition' or an 'essay' on a given topic, either in an examination or in a similar situation. That is, it is assumed that the students have no special motivation for writing about the topic and that they have not been given any special preparation for it through, for example, a class discussion, as suggested in 9.1. It should be noted, however, that we are not concerned with 'recipes' or 'formulas' for writing model compositions or essays but with procedures such as outlining, drafting and improving drafts. These form part of *any* writing task for which the students have not been helped with the actual structuring of the text they have to produce. For example, for the writing activities derived from the simulation in 8.3, the students are given both the 'content' and the format (article, letter, report, etc.) which they have to use, but they have to *organise* the data for themselves. Many students in fact write less well than they are able to simply because these or similar procedures have not been sufficiently stressed.

It is not claimed that there is any one way of going about the writing of a text (this was acknowledged in 1.1). What is important, however, is that students should appreciate the importance, for example, of making notes and drafting. They must accept that this is a *normal* part of writing. The fact that they cannot always do this when they are asked to write against the clock in an examination does not invalidate the procedures.

For the purpose of illustrating these procedures, a particularly uninspiring composition topic has been chosen: *Describe a place which seems much more neglected and sad than when it was new*.

In attempting to write about a topic like this, we are immediately faced with two problems: *who* we are writing for, which, as we have seen, naturally influences *how* we write, and *what* to write about. In normal circumstances the first problem would never arise at all, since, outside the classroom, we do not write unless there is some reason for doing so. For this type of writing, students are often exhorted to 'imagine' a reader. This may to some extent be helpful if the students also think of the task initially as forming part of, let us say, a letter or a report. This at least gives them some purpose for writing about the topic in the first place and can serve to stimulate some ideas on it. And if the students are to 'imagine a reader', it had best be 'other students in the class', who are at least *real* for them. Students do tend to write better if they know that other people in the class are going to read what they have written. Hence the importance of having a display board of some kind in the classroom.

In terms of procedures, then, our starting point is really the problem of *what* to write about: that is, getting some ideas on the topic. Understandably students often feel that they have nothing to say at all, although, if the task were preceded by a short class or group discussion, a number of ideas would certainly be thrown up. In the absence of this, the students need to *stimulate themselves* and this can be quite effectively done by *asking oneself questions* about the topic and *noting down any ideas* that occur. As a first step, then, it is suggested that the students should:

(a) *List possible ideas.*

One idea very often sparks off another. In any case, most people find it helpful to get *something* down on paper. It is better than staring at blank paper! Making an 'ideas' chart (see 6.3.1 and 8.3.1) is one way of getting started, and it has the added advantage of being flexible. You can expand, link, number ideas in a way that is difficult if you are making notes in a conventional way. Here, for example, are the results of trying to decide which place to write about.

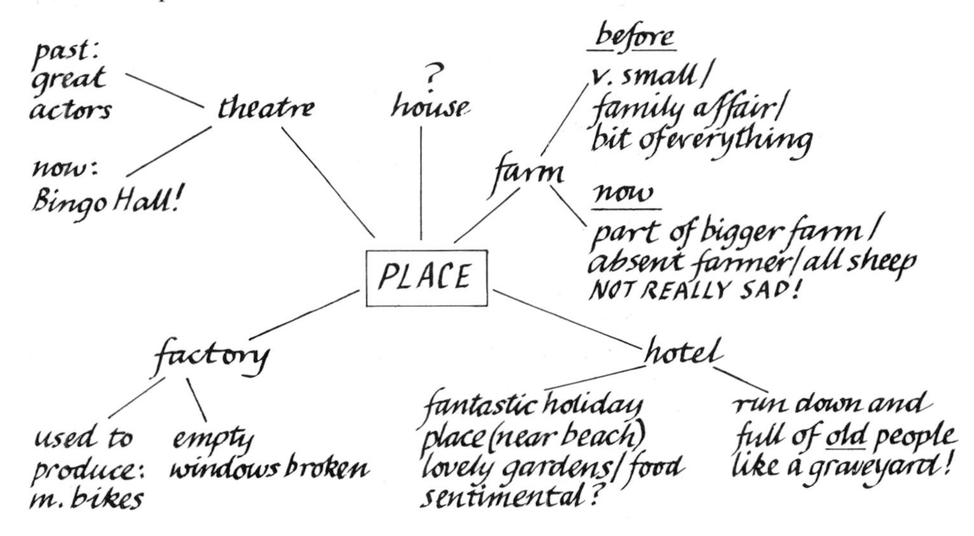

The writer played around with several ideas. *House* did not lead anywhere; *farm* did, but he decided that he was going in the wrong direction. Both *theatre* and *factory* had some potential, but in the end the writer decided that he could do more with *hotel*. However, he can easily go back and develop them later if he gets nowhere with *hotel* (and it is much easier to transfer ideas from one place to another by means of arrows).

(b) *Select and expand one idea.*

The writer has decided that he can do something with *hotel* on the basis of personal experience. Again, it helps to do this in chart form — perhaps merely expanding the first one if time is short.

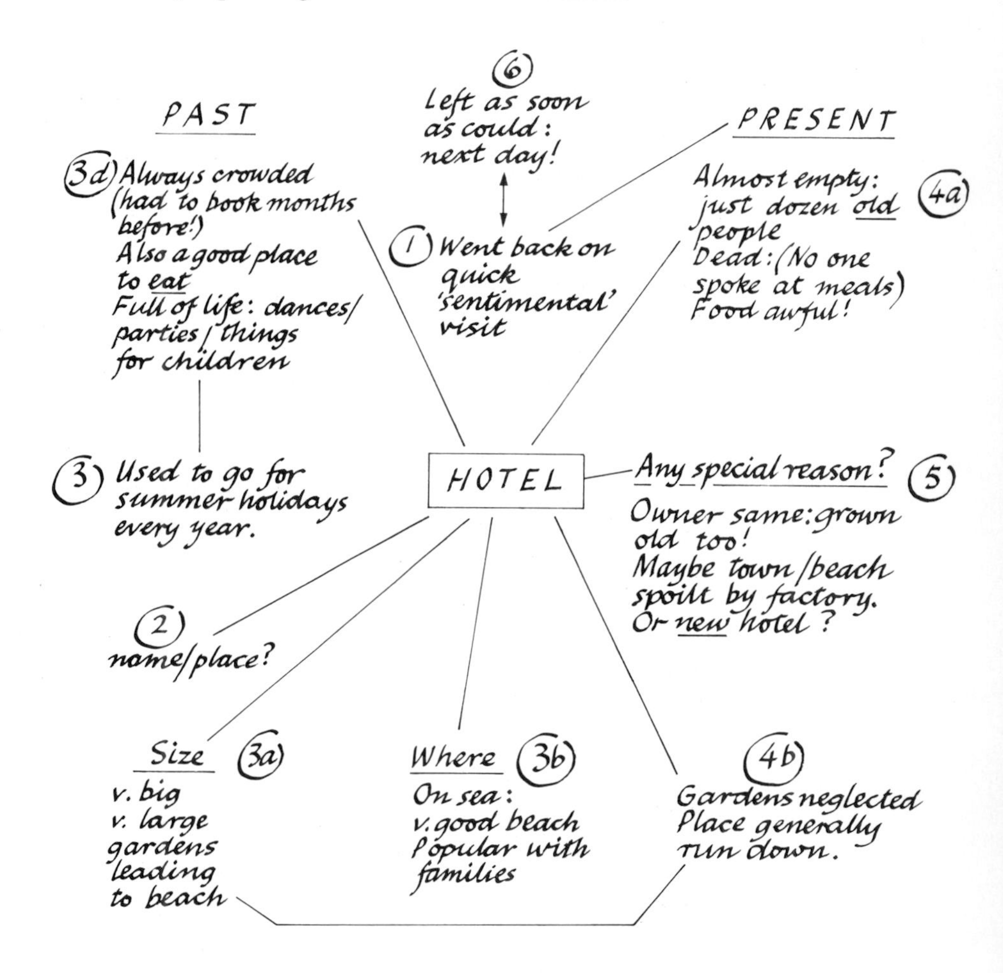


(c) *Make an outline.*

Not everyone finds it necessary or even helpful to make a plan or outline. For some it is inhibiting and prevents ideas from flowing. In any case, in some situations (such as the examination room) there may not be time. In that case, you can number the ideas in the chart in the order you think you would like to incorporate them in the text. This also ensures that nothing important is left out.

However, some students find making an outline helpful for organising ideas, especially for identifying and developing an opening and closing paragraph, which will make a great impression on the reader. Students should at least be taught how to do this, even if they do not make use of it every time they write a composition.

*Para 1 (Intro)* Went to Boxley recently - first time for 20 years - used to go with parents every summer
*Para 2* Wanted to see Seaview Hotel. Used to be best in town (new) & always booked up. Full of life: marvellous restaurant and dances. Owners arranged entertainments in garden for children.
*Para 4* Arrived in holiday season. Place almost empty!! Mostly old couples. Restaurant like cemetery! Hotel deserted by 10.
*Para 4* Everything run down: rooms needed redecorating / outside too. Garden completely neglected. Like jungle!
*Para 5 (Conclusion)* Felt place had grown old (like owners/guests). Mistake to go back. 'Escaped' next morning.

(d)
*Write a draft.*

Writing a draft is a key stage in the production of a text and the students should normally be required to do this as a matter of course. The purpose of the outline in (c) is to provide a scaffolding for the draft version. However, students should not feel that they must necessarily keep to their outline: a piece of writing sometimes 'takes off' and goes in a completely different direction, and they may find it more productive to follow this new line of development. Generally, drafts should be written quite quickly — because they will be reworked and corrected afterwards.

Not long ago I decided to go on a visit to Boxley. Our parents always used to take us to this seaside town for our summer holidays, but I had not been back there for over twenty years.

I particularly wanted to see the Seaview Hotel where we always stayed. In those days it was very new and certainly the best in town. It was always crowded during holiday season. There were parties and dances at the weekend and the owners used to arrange special entertainments for the children in the garden.

I arrived on a Saturday but the hotel was almost empty. A few more people, mostly old couples, arrived later in the day. But everywhere was so dead! People ate their food in silence and by ten o'clock the place was completely deserted.

My room depressed me: it hadn't been decorated for years. The outside of the hotel was just as bad. The gardens were completely neglected: no one bothered to cut the grass or plant flowers any more.

I felt that the place had grown old, like the people who went there! Perhaps they did not notice it. But I did. It was a mistake to go back and I decided to make my escape the following morning.

(e) *Correct and improve the draft.*

In particular the students should check for mistakes through a careful reading of what they have written. They should also review the text from the point of view of expression and organisation.

? A short time
*Not long ago I decided to go on a visit to Boxley. Our parents*
? lovely
*always used to take us to this seaside town for our summer*
20 years ago — since then
*holidays, but I had not been back there for over twenty years.*
was — curious
*I particularly wanted to see the Seaview Hotel where we*
? used to stay — the newest and
*always stayed. In those days it was very new and certainly the*
most popular hotel — very — the
*best in town. It was always crowded during holiday season.*
*There were parties and dances at the weekend and the owners*
tea and other
*used to arrange special 'entertainments' for the children*
*in the garden.*

although it was the holiday season
*I arrived on a Saturday but the hotel was almost empty. A*
? elderly
*few more people, mostly old couples, arrived later in the day.*
It was like a graveyard! — dinner — complete
*But everywhere was so dead! People ate their food in silence*
restaurant
*and by ten o'clock the ~~place~~ was completely deserted.*
I went back to my room but it
*My room depressed me: it hadn't been decorated for years!*
I went for a walk. — too
*The outside of the hotel was just as bad. The gardens were*
even — ?
*completely neglected: no one bothered to cut the grass or plant*
*flowers any more.*

It seemed to me
*~~I felt~~ that the place had grown old, like the people who*
*went there! Perhaps they did not notice it. But I did. It*
had been — as soon as I could next morning
*~~was~~ a mistake to go back and I decided to make my escape (the*
*following morning.)*

(f) *Write the final version.*

The text below is a modified version of the draft in (d). It incorporates many of the changes made in (e), but it is not just a 'fair copy' because some new ideas occurred while the final version was being written.

*A short while ago, I decided to go on a visit to Boxley, where our parents used to take us every year for our summer holidays. But that was twenty years ago - and I had not been back since then.*

*I must admit I was particularly curious to see the Seaview Hotel, where we always stayed. In those days it was the newest and by far the most popular hotel in town, always very crowded during the holiday season and full of life. There were parties and dances at the weekend, and the owners used to arrange tea and other 'entertainments' in the garden for the children. For us, of course, this was the special attraction!*

*I arrived on a Saturday and although it was the middle of the holiday season, the hotel was almost completely empty. It was a bad sign! Later in the day, a few more guests arrived. They were mostly elderly couples. At dinner, people ate in silence and by ten o'clock the hotel was completely deserted. Compared with the old days on a Saturday night, the place seemed like a graveyard!*

*I went back to my room - but that depressed me even more: it had not been decorated for years. I decided to take a walk round the garden, but this was no better. It was not just the outside of the hotel, which also needed painting. The gardens - those lovely gardens! - were completely neglected: no one bothered to plant any flowers; no one bothered even to cut the grass!*

*It seemed to me that the place had simply grown old - along with the owners and the people who went there. Perhaps they did not notice what had happened, but I did. It had been a great mistake to go back, of course, and I decided to make my escape as soon as I could in the morning.*

List possible ideas
↓
Select and expand one idea
↓
Make an outline
↓
Write a draft
↓
Correct and improve draft
↓
Write final version

To sum up, it is suggested that the students should be taught a set of procedures (summarised in the diagram), which will help them not only when they are writing about topics like the one dealt with above but also with any kind of 'free' writing. In particular, these procedures should take into account the importance of making notes, writing outlines, drafting and correcting drafts before the final version is written up. As they become more experienced, the students will no doubt want to modify these. In particular, during examinations, they may not have time to take a piece of writing through all these stages. However, the experience of having learned to make notes, to write drafts and to correct them will stand them in good stead. And they will appreciate, it is hoped, that, because it is a thinking process, writing is not just a question of 'inspiration': it also generally involves a great deal of hard work and organisation.

**Discussion**

1 In what sense is most of the writing we do in 'real life' ever really free? How useful a preparation for it is classroom composition?
2 Do you agree that there are many effective alternatives to the conventional 'composition' writing activity? What are they?
3 What is your view of the functionally-oriented writing activities suggested in 9.2?

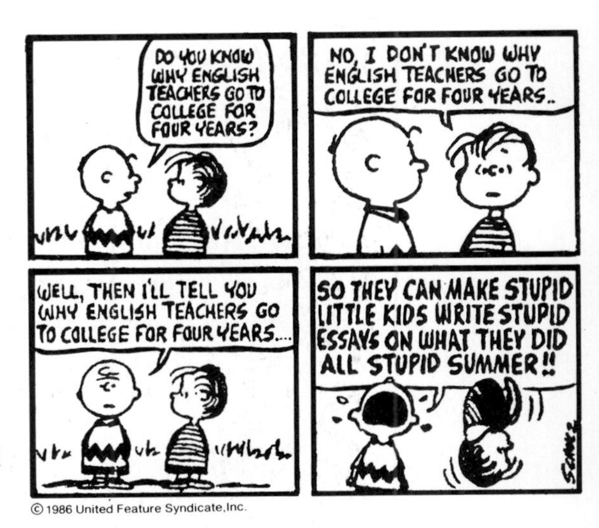



**Exercises**

1 Examine any coursebook to see what provision is made for remedial writing activities.
2 Make a list of the things you do (e.g. making notes, drafting, etc.) when you have to write, for example, a report or any complex piece of writing. Compare your procedures with a friend.
3 In the light of what you have read, make a list of what you consider to be the best twenty controlled, guided and free writing activities. Compare your 'Top Twenty' with a friend.

**References**

1 On what students do when they have to write (in the mother tongue) see S Krashen (1984) pages 12–19.
2 For writing activities at the intermediate level and beyond, see J Arnold and J Harmer *Advanced Writing Skills* (1978); N Coe et al *Writing Skills* (1983); M Carrier *Writing* (1981); E Glendinning and H Mantell *Write Ideas* (1983); J O'Driscoll *Penguin Advanced Writing Skills* (1984); D Jolly *Writing Tasks* (1984) and A Pincas *Writing in English 3* (1982).

# 10

# Correcting written work

## 10.1 Errors and mistakes

When we see something wrong with a piece of written work, we must first try to decide whether it is an error or a mistake. Broadly, learners make *errors* when they try to do something with the language which they are not yet able to do. For example, they often make false generalisations (they use a regular instead of an irregular form, such as *throwed* instead of *threw*) or they transfer from the mother tongue (they write: *The people is angry* instead of: *The people are angry*). These are two major sources of error. Mistakes, on the other hand, are slips of some kind. The students have learned something, but perhaps they have temporarily forgotten it or are tired . . . or, we feel, are just being careless.

Although in practice it is sometimes difficult to decide if something is a mistake or an error (after all, we may think we have *taught* the students something but perhaps they did not *learn* it), it is important to try to decide. Clearly, for example, if students have not learned something, we cannot expect them to correct it for themselves. On the other hand, it is perfectly reasonable and pedagogically sound to get them to correct their own mistakes. And it is certainly no use getting cross with the students if they keep on making certain errors. The lesson we can learn from these is that the students *need* to learn something, whether or not the syllabus or the coursebook has provided for it at this stage, and the best way we can help them is by giving them the opportunity to learn it. Learners' errors, in short, can help shape our teaching (and certainly our remedial teaching).

## 10.2 Teacher and student correction

It has already been suggested that we should not be unduly preoccupied with the detection and correction of mistakes in written work. *Effective* expression is not the same as *accurate* expression. Accuracy is normally measured in terms of correct grammar, spelling, etc., since these are the areas which tend to get the most attention when a piece of written work is being 'corrected'. But a piece of written work which has a number of mistakes in it may nevertheless convey the writer's communicative purpose perfectly adequately, while another piece, superficially free from mistakes, does not. The same is true of oral expression. But, as we have noted, there is a tendency to scrutinise written expression more closely because it is readily accessible to careful inspection. It is there for us to read and reread and consequently we tend to see mistakes.

Clearly, however, we cannot ignore mistakes all the time. Students expect to be informed of their progress and the correction of mistakes, by whatever procedures are used, is *one* way of doing this. Equally, however, if we indicate the ways in which a piece of writing is defective, we should also point out in what ways we think it is successful. For example, we should inform the students (not leave it to be assumed by an absence of comment) that they have made good use of connectives or punctuation devices, etc. This positive form of feedback need not add much to your work: the students can be given a checklist of items and they can see at a glance if they are making progress from the ones that have been ticked off.

Before we look at various correction procedures, we need to stress once again the importance of getting the learners themselves to identify and correct mistakes. Ultimately they will have to examine, evaluate and improve their own work: this is part of the process of drafting, correcting and writing final versions, which was described in 9.3. But this important critical ability will not develop unless the learners are given the opportunity to exercise it from a much earlier level. There will be occasions when you will want to correct all the mistakes in a piece of written work (see 10.3 for ways of doing this). Equally, however, there will be occasions when you can leave it to the students themselves. For a start, to get them into the habit of looking critically at a piece of written work which has not been corrected by the teacher, they can work in pairs or small groups to try to identify any mistakes and only then to consult with you. This procedure will not work perfectly on all occasions, but it will at least get the students into the habit of checking a piece of written work for themselves.

## 10.3 Correction procedures

Various correction procedures are examined below.

(a) *Correct all the mistakes.*

This is of course the traditional approach to the correction of written work. It is time-consuming for the teacher and discouraging for the students — at least if they get their work back covered with red ink. Apart from that, there must be some doubt about how effective this form of correction is. Some students learn nothing from it; others are more interested in why something is wrong rather than the correction itself. If you can correct something in class, while the students are still engaged in writing and everything is fresh in their minds, this is likely to be more effective than looking at a mass of corrections several days after the event.

Overall, unless the educational system obliges you to carry out this kind of correction, you should consider alternative approaches.

(b) *Correct mistakes selectively.*

That is, you do not attempt to correct all the mistakes in a piece of writing, but only those in certain areas, such as tenses or articles, either because this is where the students particularly need help or because you have decided to focus attention on these for a while. Certainly this approach is more positive than total correction — in practice, of course, most teachers exercise some form of selection — but it probably needs to be backed up by some form of remedial teaching (see below).

(c) *Indicate mistakes so that the students can correct them.*

This is normally done by underlining the mistakes and using some kind of symbol to focus the attention of the students on the kind of mistake they have made. For a possible list of these, see below.

| SYMBOL | MEANING | EXAMPLE |
|---|---|---|
| S | Incorrect spelling | *I recieved jour letter.* |
| W. O. | Wrong word order | *We know well this city.*<br>*Always I am happy here.* |
| T | Wrong tense | *If he will come, it will be too late.* |
| C | Concord Subject and verb do not agree | *Two policemen has come.*<br>*The news are bad today.* |
| WF | Wrong form | *We want that you come.*<br>*That table is our.* |
| S/P | Singular or plural form wrong | *We need more informations.* |
| ʎ | Something has been left out | *They said ʎ was wrong.*<br>*He hit me on ʎ shoulder.* |
| [ ] | Something is not necessary | *It was too [much] difficult.* |
| ?M | Meaning is not clear | *Come and rest with us for a week.*<br>*The view from here is very suggestive.* |
| NA | The usage is not appropriate | *He requested me to sit down.* |
| P | Punctuation wrong | *Whats your name*<br>*He asked me what I wanted?* |

Using a list of this kind, you can get the students, individually, in pairs or in small groups, to identify at least most of the mistakes for themselves. If they cannot, then they should consult you. This approach certainly makes them more aware of the kind of mistakes they are making and is therefore likely to result in something being learned. You do not need of course to indicate all the mistakes. In practice, however, it does not solve all the problems. For example, if students are left to identify mistakes for themselves, they may not bother. Even if they work in groups, some form of confirmation may be needed and this could take up a lot of class time in a large class.

If your teaching situation permits, you could try to implement a staged approach for getting the students to correct their own work.

*Stage 1* Underline the mistake and diagnose it by writing the appropriate symbol in the margin.

*Stage 2* Underline the mistake but do not diagnose it.

*Stage 3* Diagnose the mistake by writing the symbol in the margin but do not show where it is in the line.

*Stage 4* Put a cross in the margin (for each mistake).

*Stage 5* Put a cross against each line with a mistake but do not indicate how many mistakes there are.

(d) *Let the students identify and correct their own mistakes.*

This is not a procedure that you are likely to be able to follow all the time. Occasionally, however, you should be prepared to hand over the whole business of correction to the students — which they will generally do scrupulously and with enjoyment.

Other things you can do to help students when they make mistakes are:

(a) *Explain a mistake.*

For example, you can write a comment in the margin or at the end of a piece of written work. This procedure is especially useful for drawing attention to recurrent mistakes in a particular area and when you are able to look at students' work in class.

(b) *Indicate to the students that they should consult you about a mistake.*

This may be used as an alternative to (b) and (c) above. Very often the students themselves can suggest the correction when their attention has been drawn to a mistake.

(c) *Use the mistake as a basis for remedial teaching.*

This procedure should be followed if a sufficient number of students in the class have made a mistake to warrant general correction. Alternatively, you can set individual remedial work. Remedial teaching may take the form of an explanation, where this is felt to be sufficient, or exercises, oral or written, whichever seems to be appropriate, designed to correct the mistake.

Teachers tend to place their faith in one type of correction procedure rather than another. In particular, many do not accept (or only accept with some misgiving) self-correction procedures. In general, however, although it is important to give the students opportunities to correct written work so that they develop a self-critical attitude, it does not seem that one approach is so intrinsically superior that it can be used all the time and you should therefore draw on the various approaches to suit the needs of your students.

**Discussion**

1 Do you think that the distinction made between errors and mistakes is important?
2 From your own experience of teaching (or learning), do you think that detailed teacher correction of written work is effective? Give your reasons.
3 In medium to large sized classes (i.e. over 30 students), what problems do you see in getting students to correct their own work?

**Exercises**

1 Devise your own set of correction procedures. You can modify the list on page 125.
2 Use your correction symbols to indicate the mistakes in the following piece of writing, which is in the form of a letter.

9

My dear, how are you. I am very good but am very much tried in these days, perhaps I ask that the doctor visit me quickly (but I no like going at doctors!)
Someting I must to tell you. I change employ within a little and I go to work in bank. I am much exciting for this! I hope to gain more at bank.
Let me to have all your news. I am crazy to know them. Believe me, I remain,

Your freind,
Paolo

**References**

1 For useful general guidance on correction see RJ Wingfield (1975). For student correction see CJ Brumfit in S Holden (1983) *Correcting written work*. The ideas in this chapter owe a good deal to these two articles. See also R White (1980) pages 106–9 and J Harmer (1983) pages 140–1.
2 For correction symbols see J Willis (1981) pages 172–3 and L Dangerfield in A Matthews et al (eds) (1985) pages 195–8.

# A boy wrote a poem

**NICHOLAS CHAPMAN**

A boy wrote a poem,
It was from homework from class,
He wrote about cliff-tops,
And how the winds pass.
He just let it flow
from his head to his pen,
But his spelling was bad,
"C, do this again!"

A boy wrote a poem,
And thought of his mark.
And this time he checked it
And wrote of the dark.
He changed and corrected,
Gave it in the next day,
He got "B + Good effort"
and threw it away.

*Nicholas Chapman is 12 and attends Queen Katherine School, Kendal, Cumbria.*
Published in the Times Educational Supplement 16.8.85.

# 11

# Writing activities for children

## 11.1 Reasons for teaching writing

The age group we have in mind here is that of pupils about 7–8 years old, who have only recently started elementary school. Since children at this age are good at learning orally and are still learning to write in their mother tongue, we need to explain and perhaps justify why we should want to teach them to write in another language at this stage, apart from perhaps just giving them a few routine copying exercises. Won't it just be yet another learning burden for them? If it were, then it might be better to keep writing to an absolute minimum. But it does not have to be a burden, as we shall see when we look at the various types of activity proposed, especially if we keep in mind the many good reasons there are for teaching writing at this age. Some of these apply to learners of all ages. A number, however, are peculiar to children.

(a) Children usually *enjoy* writing. This is partly because they have only just started to write in their mother tongue. Even activities like copying still have a certain novelty value.

(b) Most children *expect* to be taught to write (and read of course). This is one of the things you have to do when you go to school and they see it as part of learning a language.

(c) Children, like older students — but even more so, *need a break* from oral work. They enjoy talking, of course, but they soon get tired, even if you keep changing the activities. Writing activities provide a very important quiet (or relatively quiet!) period for them in the lesson, after which they usually return to oral work refreshed and less restless.

(d) Writing gives children an opportunity to *work at their own pace*, which is very relaxing for them. Remember that there can be very big differences between learners at this age because their motor skills are still developing.

(e) Access to the written language sometimes *clears up difficulties* which children have when learning orally. Sometimes they cannot tell you about these difficulties because they are not even aware of them themselves.

(f) Writing activities provide an *opportunity for personal contact*. This again is very important for learners of this age, who are still getting used to the classroom environment. When they are writing, you can go and work with them individually (at least with those who need and want this attention), sort out difficulties and encourage them. This is sometimes more important than the writing activity itself.

(g) Children *like and need to have a record* of many of the things they do in the classroom — of dialogues they have practised and songs they have sung. Again this is important because, although they learn quickly, they forget quickly too. You should not forget that they lead very busy lives — in and out of school!

(h) Children need the *extra language contact* that writing can provide, especially through some sort of homework activity. This is essential if there is a long gap between one lesson and the next. Homework, of course, need not be a burden. For example, if children are asked to illustrate a song (see 11.2.1 (i) below), this will help to keep them in touch with the language (they are very likely to be heard singing it to themselves as they draw!) as well as being enjoyable.

(i) Children need *something to show their parents*. Parents are usually pleased when they hear their children utter a few words in a foreign language but they are usually more convinced that they are making progress (even perhaps if they are not) if they have tangible evidence in the form of written work. They usually *expect* homework to be in the form of writing too.

### 11.1.1 Some guidelines for teaching writing to children

The main purpose for going into the reasons for teaching children of this age to write is that they will help us to see how we should go about it. Two things especially should be kept in mind. First, writing must not impair oral fluency. There is no reason why this should happen provided the pupils get plenty of opportunities for hearing and using English and if writing is treated as an extension of oral work. Secondly, we should not try to teach aspects of the written language which learners at this age cannot be expected to understand and cope with. For example, they are too young to do sentence linking activities (except in the few instances that these can be turned into a kind of game) and the kind of texts they write are more likely to be imaginative than coherent. Remember that the pupils are still learning how to organise their ideas in their mother tongue.

(a) *Give the pupils plenty of opportunities for copying.*

This will help them feel at ease with the written language and should also provide them with records of things they may need, e.g. lists of words, copies of songs, poems and dialogues.

(b) *Give the pupils adequate opportunities to use orally learned language in writing.*

In short, they will need a fair amount of controlled practice, particularly to reinforce key structures and vocabulary. This need not and should not be boring. (In fact, most workbooks for children try to make this type of activity interesting and enjoyable.)

(c) *Provide activities which the pupils can do at their own speed.*

Some pupils will finish an activity very quickly (and call out for attention!). You should be prepared to extend the activity (by some form of parallel writing) or have an extra activity ready (which need not be a written one). Slower pupils should as far as possible always be given the opportunity to finish an activity in some form (that is, they must not be left feeling that they have failed, otherwise they may begin to get discouraged).

(d) *Work with the pupils wherever possible.*

Writing activities provide a break for the pupils — but not, as a rule, for the teacher! Some pupils will actually *need* your help. With all of them writing will provide an opportunity to get to know them a little better personally.

(e) *Make sure that the pupils begin to see writing as a means of communication.*

This can be done mainly by getting the pupils to write to one another in class (see 11.2.3 and 11.2.4), which is an activity the learners particularly enjoy at this age.

(f) *Encourage the pupils to be creative.*

This should balance controlled and language-focused activities suggested in (b). At this age they have plenty of imagination and they should be encouraged to use it.

(g) *Make writing activities enjoyable.*

This is the most important provision. Remember that many pupils are just starting on a programme which may last for years. It would be a pity if they were turned off at this early age through boredom or failure. You must try, therefore, to ensure that they get as much fun out of writing as they do from other activities.

### 11.1.2 The organisation of written work

See also 4.1.3. At this age the pupils will normally be making use of workbooks or activity books. This in itself will help to keep together a good deal of their written work. Sometimes, however, material has to be cut out and a folder will be useful for keeping together this and other looseleaf material.

As a rule at this age it is better to ask pupils to work with exercise books (rather than a folder for everything). The kind of exercise book they use (i.e. the distance between the lines) may also be important for writing. Pupils will need at least two exercise books: one for vocabulary lists and related activities (e.g. Word Bingo) and the other for copies of dialogues, songs and poems, which they should be encouraged to illustrate. They may also need one for project work such as making an illustrated dictionary.

## 11.2 Writing activities

These have been divided into four groups — copying, practice with words, practice with sentences and creative writing — but there is inevitably some overlap between these groups.

11.2.1
Copying

(a) *Joining up dots to form words*

This very basic activity can be useful in the early stages, partly to give the pupils practice in forming the letters. More than that, however, it gives the pupils the illusion that they are producing the words for themselves. It is of course an activity they are familiar with through puzzle books that contain hidden objects in pictures.

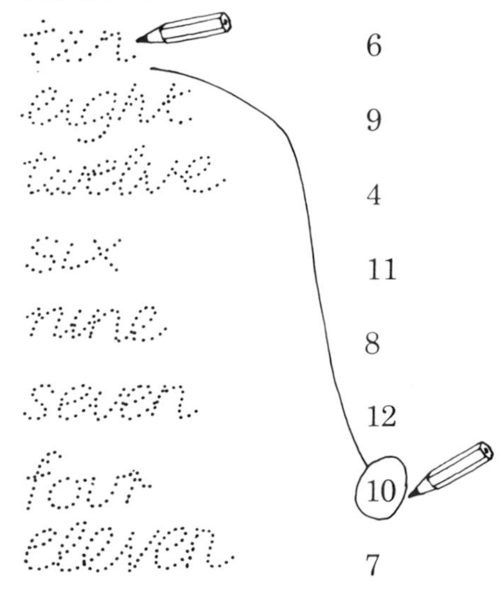


(b) *Finding the word that is different*

The pupils are given sets of 4–5 words like those in the diagram and are asked to find and write out the word that is different. This combines reading with writing. Children enjoy the problem-solving aspect of this activity.

cat banana dog horse
red yellow man green

(c) *Labelling items*

For this the pupils use words listed for them in a box to identify and label, for example, individual objects, people in a group, objects in a scene, etc.

| | |
|---|---|
| bird | lorry |
| cat | pig |
| cow | tractor |
| donkey | tree |
| house | woman |

(d) *Completing crossword puzzles*

The pupils use or select words from a list to complete simple crossword puzzles like these. The puzzles can be more extensive as the pupils progress.

black
blue
brown
green
orange
red

(e) *Finding words*

The pupils have to find and write out words which have been 'hidden' in boxes like the one below. The words may belong to a set (e.g. animals, clothes, etc.) and at a later stage may form a sentence, such as an instruction. The pupils can also make their own wordboxes, working individually or in groups, using words which they have been given.

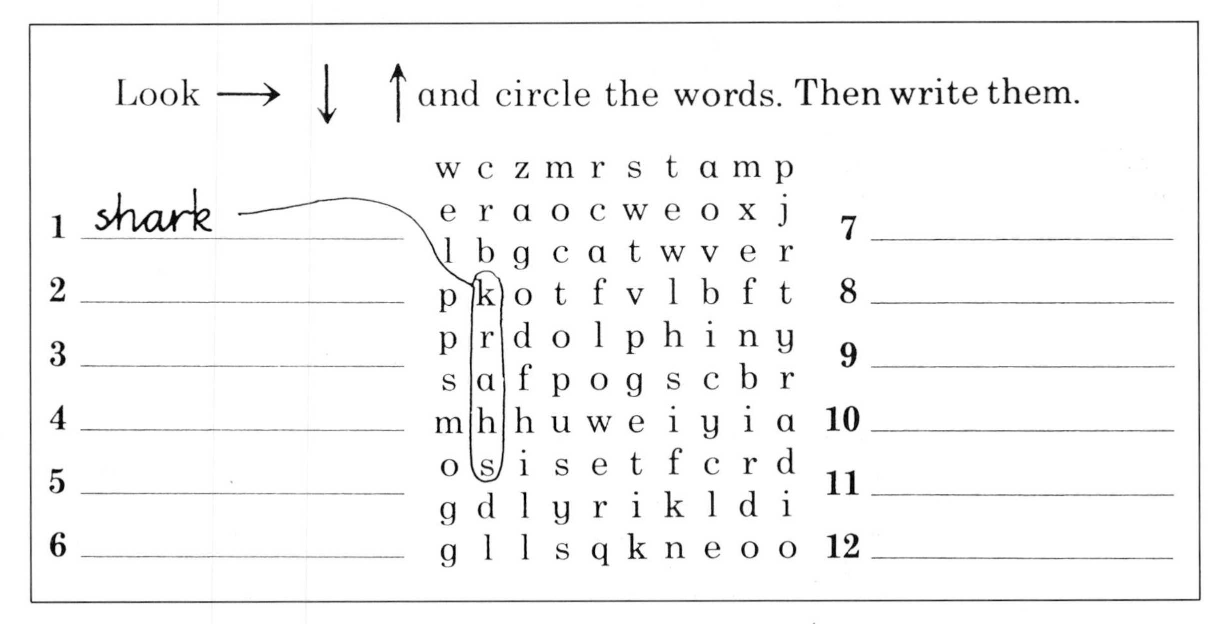


(f) *Filling in speech bubbles*

The pupils have to fill in speech bubbles by matching the sentences with the situation. The activity is more interesting if the pictures form a sequence.

(g) *Forming dialogues or stories from jumbled sentences*

See 4.3.1 (c) for this activity. This makes a good pairwork or group activity and can be based on something the pupils have already heard.

(h) *Playing word bingo*

See 4.2.3 (e) for this activity. This is a key activity for learners at this level because vocabulary sets need to be kept fresh in their minds through constant revision. It helps with pronunciation as well as spelling, because the pupils can tell you which words to write on the board and then hear you read them out. You can also play 'phrase bingo' with the pupils, but be careful that this does not present problems for slow copiers.

| | |
|---|---|
| a green car | |
| a black hat | |
| a blue pen | |
| a red book | |
| | |

(i) *Making copies of songs, etc.*

The pupils make their own copies of dialogues, songs and poems (i.e. any key reference material) in a book set aside for this purpose and provide their own illustrations. This again is a very important activity. Most pupils exhibit a good deal of imagination when illustrating material of this kind.

11.2.2
Word activities

For the activities in this section the pupils have to provide (i.e. think of and spell) the words they need.

(a) *Completing crosswords*

This is similar to 11.2.1 (d) except that the pupils are not given any of the words. They may, however, be given picture clues (perhaps placed next to or linked to the relevant squares to be filled in).

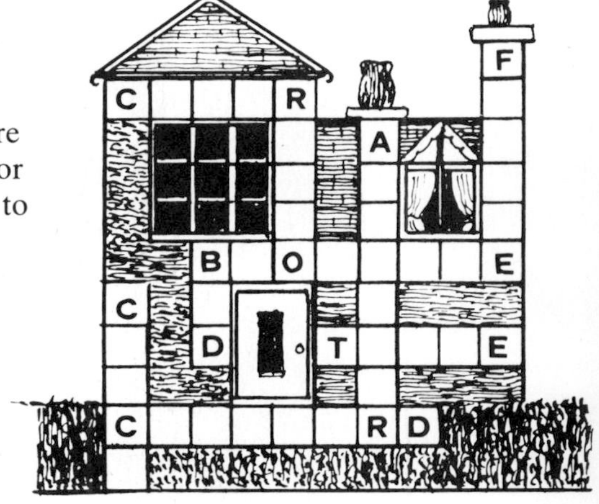

(b) *Labelling items*

This is similar to 11.2.1 (c), except that the pupils have to provide the words. They can also be asked to draw or complete the pictures needed. For example, they may be asked to label items in a zoo or fridge which they have drawn.

(c) *Making lists*

For example, the pupils may be asked to compile lists of:

— things they would like to eat;
— countries they would like to visit;
— animals they would like to see (or have as pets) (etc.)

They can then compare their choices with a friend.

I would like to have
(1) a small dog
(2) two elephants
(3) a long snake
(4) a parrot

(d) *Classifying items*

The pupils have to identify and then arrange in categories (the headings will normally have to be provided or at least worked out with the class beforehand) things that they can see in a picture.

| animals | people | clothes |
| --- | --- | --- |
| dog<br>horse | man<br>girl | hat<br>trousers<br>jacket |

(e) *Completing texts*

That is, the pupils put in the missing words. The texts can be dialogues they have practised, stories accompanied by a picture sequence or songs, poems and riddles which they have heard (etc.).

Sally goes round the .....,
Sally goes round the .....,
Sally goes round the .....
on a Saturday .....!

(f) *Correcting sentences or texts*

These should be accompanied by a picture so that the pupils are correcting mistakes of fact (not grammar). For example:

There is a boat in the picture.
There are two boats ..............................

A girl is going home. She's got a bottle in her hand.
A boy is going home. He ..............................

(g) *Making words*

The pupils are given one long word and, working in pairs or small groups, see how many new words they can make from it. They sometimes like to look through books to try to find words (and this is a good way of getting them interested in class readers).

COMPETITION

pet
note
come
time

(h) *Making notes*

This is particularly important during a game when they may need to keep a record of what objects they have won or which animals they have seen (if the game takes them to a zoo or a safari park). Usually the items to be noted are words, but sometimes phrases have to be written down. If much writing is involved, pupils should work in pairs (i.e. one actually playing, the other making notes) so as not to slow the game down.

We have seen these animals

1 a giraffe
2 a mother tiger and a baby tiger
3 five long snakes and one fat snake

### 11.2.3 Sentence activities

The purpose of these activities is to reinforce key items of structure (often together with a good deal of vocabulary). There is no reason why this kind of manipulative practice need be boring (in any case most children enjoy repetition). Most workbooks provide good activities for this kind of practice, but you may need to supplement this. In any case the suggestions below will help you to see if the workbook has left out any useful areas of activity.

(a) *Writing parallel texts*

That is, the pupils have a model and have to write one or more parallel versions. This is particularly useful if the pupils write dialogues which they can then practise with one another. Later on, they can be asked to write short narrative sequences (5–6 sentences) which will give them some practice in basic sentence linking (*and, but, so*) and sequencing (*first, then, after that*).

(b) *Completing speech bubbles*

This is like 11.2.1 (f), except that the pupils now have to supply the sentences for themselves.

(c) *Writing sentence sequences*

This is a device for getting the pupils to write sentences using the same structure. For example, they use the days of the week to write about themselves or perhaps a character from their coursebook. Although this involves repetition, there is always room for imagination!

It's Monday. I'd like to go to China!
It's Tuesday. I'd like to go to Australia!
It's Wednesday. I'd like to go to the moon!

It's raining. I'm going to go swimming.
It's windy. I'm going to go flying.

(d) *Compiling information*

For this activity the pupils have to write some sentences which provide information, for example, about one of the characters in the coursebook or about a topic. It often involves repetition of a structure (and can be used just for that purpose) and may be done with reference to a picture.

Notice that in the examples below the pupils also practise incidentally pronominal reference.

Professor Patent's got a telescope.
He's got a cat and a dog.
He's also got a monster!

Professor Patent's got a gramophone
He's also got a television
He's got a big pie!

(e) *Completing questionnaires*

For this the pupils work with questionnaires that have been prepared for them. It can be a useful way of disguising some very basic question practice. The pupils can of course use such questionnaires to question one another.

DO YOU KNOW THE ANSWERS?

1 What do monkeys eat?
..............................
2 Where do they live?
..............................
3 Can they swim?

ASK A FRIEND!

1 When do you get up in the morning?
..................................
2 What do you eat for breakfast?
..................................

(f) *Making notes*

This is similar to keeping records while playing a game. Many activities involve keeping some kind of record in the form of a list. For example, the pupils can be asked to write down, in sentence form, the differences between two pictures or the number of mistakes they can find in a picture.

(g) *Writing questionnaires*

This is similar to (e) above except that the pupils have to write the questionnaires as well. See 4.6 (a) and (b) for details. Young learners enjoy testing one another! You must, however, check that they can answer the questions themselves. Also, when interviewing, because they are slower at writing than adolescents and adults, they need time to record answers and preferably should sit down to do this so that they write neatly.

(h) *Recording personal information*

Young learners like talking and writing about themselves and they will very happily write down personal data (names, age, address, family details, etc.) or make lists of their possessions or likes and dislikes. The activity can be used for some elementary sentence linking practice.

I've got a television in my bedroom.
I've also got a lot of books and a lot of toys.
I've got a rabbit but it's in the garden.

My favourite month is August because it's a holiday.
My favourite colour is blue because I like the sea.
I don't like snakes and I don't

(i) *Writing notes*

See 4.5, where this activity is described in detail. That is, the pupils write to one another (and to you) in class. This is a key activity for young learners because it gets them to write quickly. Thus in five minutes they can get a lot of writing practice sending and answering notes. For sentence practice (see 11.2.4 (a) for more creative writing) the pupils can:

— ask for something (e.g. one of a number of picture cards which another pupil has in front of him);
— ask for some personal information;
— ask about a character in the coursebook, etc.

### 11.2.4 Creative writing activities

Pupils at this age need plenty of opportunities to use language imaginatively. Unlike many older learners, they are always willing to show you their work and to ask 'Can I say this?', so that fewer mistakes occur than might be expected. Let pupils work together in pairs or small groups wherever possible.

(a) *Writing notes*

See 11.2.3 (i). For this activity, however, give them tasks that will require longer sequences. For example:

Friday
Dear Elena,
Please draw me a picture of a monster. It has big eyes and long teeth and there is fire in its mouth. It has a very long tail. Thank you.
Jorge

Dear Hans,
Go to the front of the classroom. Stand on a chair. Then sing Happy Birthday!
Yours,
Irma

(b) *Writing about pictures*

See 4.6 (i) for the basic idea behind this activity. Choose pictures that will encourage the pupils to use fantasy and rehearse the idea orally first so that they understand the kind of thing you want. Pupils can also draw pictures for one another to write about.

(c) *Writing rolecards*

See 4.6 (f) for a description of this activity. The pupils can ask someone to be a character from the coursebook or an animal!

For Carlo!
You are Tricky Dicky. You are a very bad man. You steal things. You are very unhappy.

For Dora!
You are a cat. You eat a lot and you are very fat. You cannot run and you cannot climb. You like sleeping.

(d) *Making up stories*

See for example 4.6 (e). You can start by asking the pupils to write short dialogues, with two speakers, which they should then cut up and give to another group to piece together. Then let them try their hand at very simple stories (5–6 sentences), which they should also cut up for another group to piece together.

(e) *Writing notices*

See 7.3.8 (b). You can give the pupils small picture cards for this activity or let them use their own ideas (i.e. they may prefer to write about things they would actually like or things they have). Children very often like to exchange things so the activity can be authentic. The pupils can also write rules and regulations for their classroom, for example, or for a club or recreation park.

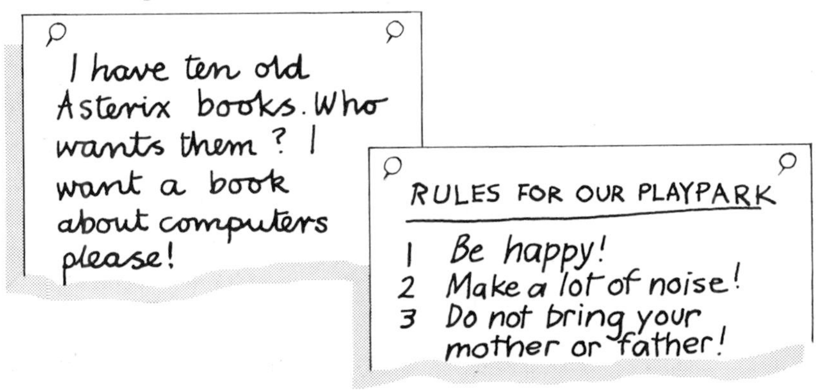


(f) *Writing book reports*

See 5.5.2 (d). When the pupils have reached the stage of using class readers — or even looking through them — they can be asked to write 2–3 sentence 'reports' on them. The reports should be pasted at the back of the book for other pupils to read.

> It's a very good book. I like it. But it is sad. It is about a girl and

> I like the pictures in this book, but the story is not very interesting. I can't finish it.

(g) *Writing messages*

See 7.3.8 (c) for the basic idea. The pupils will happily enter into writing messages from other strange places: the moon, the bottom of the sea, a balloon, the middle of the desert, etc.

> Dear Mum and Dad,
> I am under the sea! It is wet here and there are many big fish. I have a lot of friends. One friend is an octopus. He is taking this letter for me!

Writing messages can also be done in postcard form (see 7.3.8 (j)) and they can also be written in code.

*Write out the complete code.*
A = V  C = X  E = Z
B = W  D = Y
*Then write messages like this.*

HJIYVT

YZVM IDXF,
DO'N HT WDMOCYVT JI
NVOPMYVT KGZVNZ XJHZ
OJ HT KVMOT
TJPMN,
VIIV

Don't forget to get your pupils to send birthday messages when it is someone's birthday. The preparation of the card can be done as homework.

Make a birthday card for a friend. Draw a picture and write a message.

Many Happy Returns of the Day!

Happy Birthday to you!

A Very Happy Birthday!

Very Best Wishes for your Birthday!

(h) *Project work*

One useful and enjoyable project for learners at this age is to get them to make their own picture dictionaries. The pupils can work on their own or in groups (even if they work in groups, so as to help one another, they may like to make their own copy). For the dictionary, they will need an exercise book. They can draw their own pictures or cut suitable ones out of magazines. The intention is not to get them to keep a record of all or even many of the words they have learnt but only to write about items that interest them. They should write sentences about their words (not definitions) and from time to time go back and add to what they have written.



Most pupils also enjoy making a class wallsheet (see 5.5.2 (g)), which will provide a focus for a number of writing activities, e.g. little stories, captions and balloons for pictures, jokes and riddles (etc.). Both the picture dictionary and the wallsheet should be spread over a school year (unless the pupils are working intensively, e.g. on a summer course).

Many of the projects suggested in 8.2.2 can easily be adapted for younger learners.

**Discussion**

1 Do you think it is either necessary or desirable to teach young learners to write in a foreign language?
2 Would you give children opportunities for creative writing early on in the course or would you restrict them (for example) to copying and reinforcement activities?
3 What are the things you would do to make sure that children really enjoy writing?
4 How important do you think it is to ensure that children's written work is neat and tidy?

**Exercises**

1 Examine any children's course to see what provision is made for writing activities. Is there a workbook? If so, are the writing activities (a) interesting (b) useful?
2 Suggest other activities for each of the four sections 11.2.1–11.2.4.
3 Make a list of the projects in 8.2.2 which could be adapted for children and work out how you would develop one of them.

**References**

1 On teaching young learners to write see O Dunn (1984) and S Holden (ed) (1980).
2 For a range of writing activities, see D Byrne *Roundabout Resource Book* and related Workbooks (Modern English Publications); M Iggulden et al *Sam on Radio 321* (Longman); K Johnson *Now for English* (Nelson); *Kaleidoscope* (MacMillan) and *Snap!* (Heinemann).
3 The illustrations in 11.2.1 (a) and (e) are from *Sam on Radio 321*; the illustration in 11.2.1 (f) has been adapted from *Kaleidoscope*; the illustrations in 11.2.1 (c) and (d); 11.2.2 (a) and (f); 11.2.3 (i) and 11.2.4 (a) are from the *Roundabout Workbooks*.

# 12

# Teaching the English script

## 12.1 The needs of the learners

All students whose native language does not use the Latin script will have to be taught the symbols needed for writing English. In some circumstances you may also want to improve the handwriting of those who already use the Latin script.

In order to be able to do this effectively and, no less important, sympathetically, you will need to inform yourself of the learners' areas of difficulty. Four possible 'problem areas' are noted below.

(a) The students have to learn the shapes of the new symbols. This is not just a question of teaching the letters of the English alphabet, the order of which is mainly irrelevant for teaching purposes. Instead, some decision has to be taken how to group the symbols together for effective practice, taking into account features which allow comparison and contrast. For example, the letter *a* may be derived from the letter *c*; the letters *a* and *o*, on the other hand, need to be contrasted.

(b) The students have to learn two sets of symbols: lower and upper case (that is, small letters and capitals). Again, a decision has to be made whether to teach both sets of symbols together or whether to teach first the small letters and then the capitals.

(c) The students may have to learn to write in a new direction: that is, from left to right instead of from right to left. This will only apply to certain groups of learners (for example, to Arab students but not to those whose native language employs one of the Devanagari scripts of the North Indian languages). This physical aspect of mastering the new script is not to be underestimated.

(d) The students may have to learn the position of the symbols of the script in relation to the ruled lines. Essentially the English script may be viewed as sitting on the line and extending upwards and downwards, while the symbols in the Devanagari scripts, for example, 'hang' from the line above.

Another key factor will, of course, be the age of the learners. Adult learners will want (and will probably need) to learn more quickly and will therefore require concentrated practice, which to a large extent, given the right guidance, they can provide for themselves out of class. For children, the programme should be spread over a much longer period. While it is assumed that they will already have mastered their native language script, they will probably still have some handwriting difficulties and not all their motor skills will be equally well developed. Hence the need for copying activities as suggested in 11.2.1. Young learners will also benefit a good deal from handwriting activities that give them the opportunity to play, and they will almost certainly need some kind of workbook.

## 12.2 Letter shapes

For the purpose of teaching the shapes of the new symbols, we need to identify groups of letters which can be effectively and conveniently taught together. Various groupings have been proposed (see notes on sources). One, for example, proposes ten groups, as shown below. Upper and lower case letters are taught together, integrated with punctuation practice.

| | |
|---|---|
| 1 i, l, t | 6 f, s, r |
| 2 v, w, b | 7 c, e, o |
| 3 u, y (+ ? and !) | 8 a, d, g |
| 4 n, m, h | 9 j, q, x |
| 5 k, p (+ . and ,) | 10 z (+ numerals) |

Another approach has eight groups, each identified by a letter, for the lower case symbols.

| | |
|---|---|
| 1 the *e* group: e, i, u, t | 5 the *r* group: r, s |
| 2 the *c* group: c, a, d | 6 the *l* group: l, h, k, f, b |
| 3 the *o* group: o, w | 7 the *j* group: j, p, y |
| 4 the *n* group: n, m, x, v | 8 the *z* group: z, g, p |

Capitals are taught separately and are divided into the following nine groups:

| | | | |
|---|---|---|---|
| 1 C, O, Q, A, E | 4 P, R, B | 7 I, J | |
| 2 N, M, K, H | 5 D, L | 8 S, G | |
| 3 U, V, W, X | 6 T, F | 9 Y, Z | numerals |

Awareness of groupings such as these is useful if you want to do remedial work in certain areas (for example, you may find that some students are consistently miswriting or confusing some symbols).

## 12.3 Procedures for teaching script

At the start, most students will need to be made aware of some of the important differences between writing the English script and writing in their native language. For this purpose, if they are asked to write something in their own language and to note some of the essential movements, a broad comparison can be made between this and writing in English. You will also need to draw attention to the positioning of the right forearm on the desk, at something like 80°, and the flexible movements of the wrist to produce anti-clockwise motions, which sometimes give students a lot of difficulty. You must be prepared to demonstrate these points. Two 'warm up' activities should also be noted:

(a) *Rhythmic patterns*

To get the students used to some of the characteristic shapes of the English script and the movements needed for making them, you can ask them to draw rhythmic patterns like those shown below. They are particularly important for students who are having to learn to write from left to right (for whom even drawing horizontal lines across the page is a useful activity). Rhythmic patterns can relate to some of the basic shapes of the letters, as in the example below:

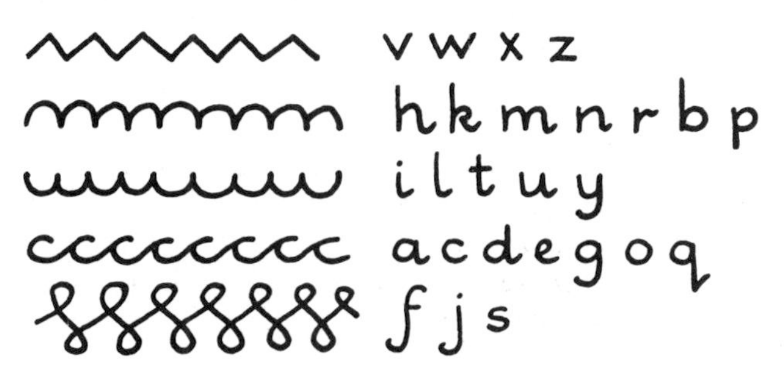


Many teachers prefer to get their students to draw these patterns on blank paper. For children the activity can be presented as a game, such as climbing up and down mountains.

(b) *Writing in air*

It generally helps, whatever the age of the students, to practise tracing the *shape* of the letters in the air. This helps them to concentrate on the way a letter is formed and enables them to go on practising as long as they like.

For this activity draw a large version of the letter on the board, with arrows indicating the directions to be followed, and then demonstrate the movements yourself. The students can make large movements first of all, gradually making smaller ones. Students who are accustomed to writing from left to right can be helped by being asked to make a series of strokes or circles which start on the left and move towards the right.

The example below shows how letter formation in the air can be presented in a fun-like way for children:

With your finger, follow the mice.

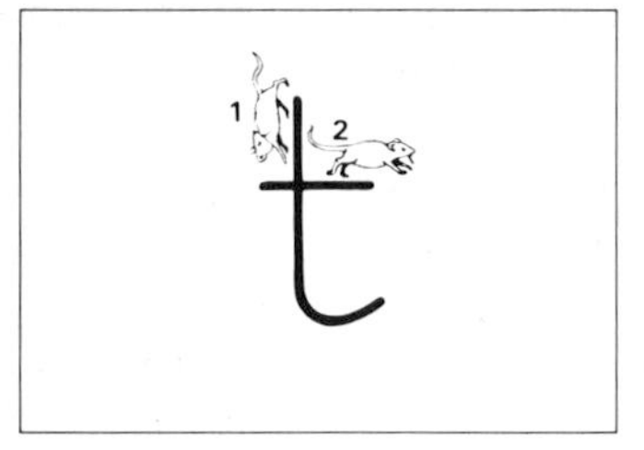


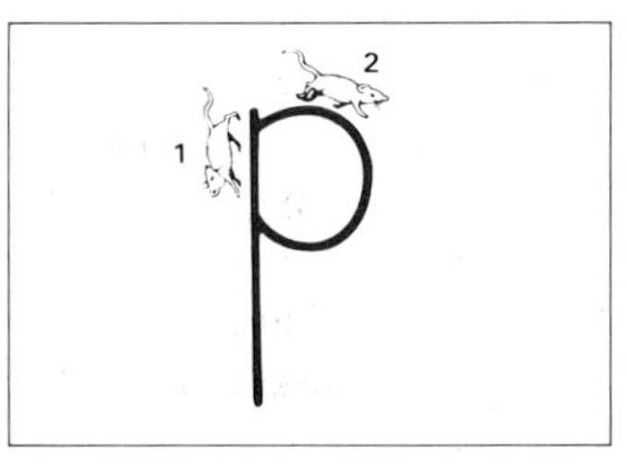


**12.3.1 Some basic procedures for teaching script**

(a) *Give the students clear and carefully made models to follow.*

Draw these on the board if a workbook is not available. In any case, a model on the board, drawn by you, will help to concentrate attention. You must always be prepared to *demonstrate* script.

(b) *Show the students where to begin the strokes from which each letter is made (there may be more than one stroke).*

For example:

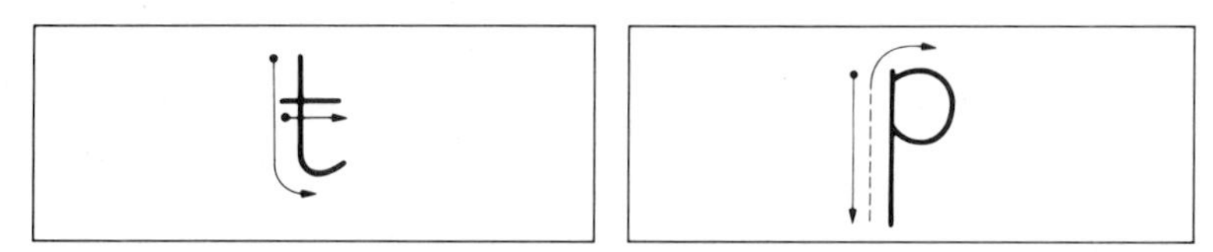


(c) *Get the students to practise several specimens of each letter.*

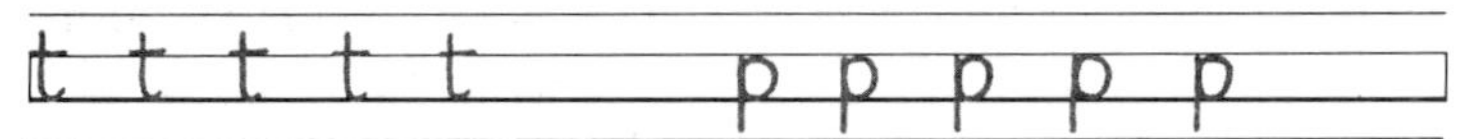


(d) *Get the students to practise the new letters in combination with previously learned ones.*

These may be simply patterns of letters or words, phrases and short sentences.

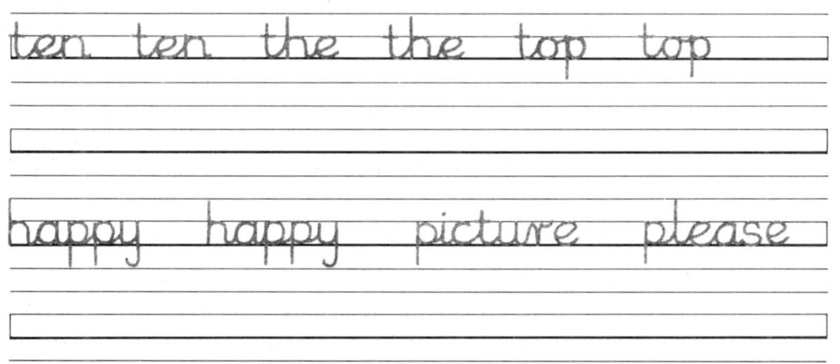


A matter which requires careful attention is the actual positioning of the symbols on the lower horizontal line. At the start it will probably help the students to practise within the limits of an additional ruled or dotted line, as shown below.

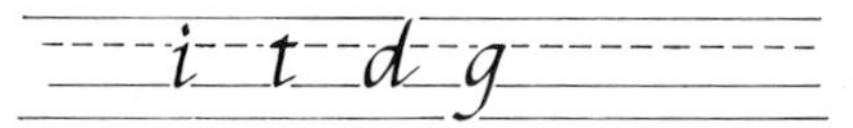


Some teachers, however, argue that any ruled lines at the start make it more difficult for the students to write well because it restricts the size of their script, and they therefore prefer blank paper.

On the whole, it would seem better to separate the teaching of capitals from lower case symbols. This permits the kind of grouping according to shape as shown in the second example on page 144. It also takes into account the many differences between a lower case letter and its upper case counterpart (for example, r and R, *g* and G).

In addition, there are some other factors which need to be considered. In the first place, we shall need to decide *how early* in the course to introduce writing practice. Should we get the students to practise making the shapes of the letters very early on, even before they can read, perhaps as a break from oral work, or should we wait until they are familiar with the symbols through some form of reading recognition practice? Although there is clearly no one answer to this question, on the whole, if there is time for this activity, which is essentially a kind of drawing exercise, it would seem a good idea to introduce the students to the mechanical problems of actually making the symbols as soon as possible. Younger learners enjoy this kind of activity, while adult students may actually *need* to have accelerated instruction in both reading and writing in order to become literate in the foreign language as quickly as possible.

The *pace* of that part of the writing programme where the students are being taught the symbols will relate to the age level of the learners. The work of younger learners, for example, should be carefully supervised in class, although this does not rule out a certain amount of practice as homework. Adult students, on the other hand, might well be given cyclostyled sheets containing appropriate copying material, so that, after an introduction to the items to be practised, they continue to work on their own out of class.

We must also decide *what kind of script* we are going to teach. Do we teach them some form of cursive writing from the start or do we delay the introduction of this until they have learned to print? Again, the age factor is relevant: younger learners are probably best taught the printed form first. On the other hand, there is no great harm in introducing from the start a kind of *modified* cursive, of a kind which is easy to write and easy to read and which stands very close to the printed form. In making a decision, we have to take the needs of the learners into account: adult students, for example, would probably be intolerant of anything less than cursive, since this is the only form they can envisage themselves using.

**Discussion**

1 Which would you prefer?
   (a) to teach capitals and lower case letters together or separately;
   (b) to teach a print script first or a modified cursive.
   Give your reasons.
2 How important is the teacher's own handwriting as a model? Would you be prepared to change yours to help your students?

**Exercises**

1 Make a list of any difficulties that your students have (or might have) with the English script.
2 Choose some of the letters of the English alphabet (capitals and lower case) and work out the strokes needed to form them.

**References**

1 Two useful articles on teaching the English script are GK Pullum (1971) and BH Seward (1972).
2 The first group of symbols on page 144 is from J Bright and R Piggott *Handwriting* (CUP 1976); the second is from BH Seward (1972).
3 Some useful materials for teaching English script are J Bright and R Piggott *Handwriting* (CUP 1976); D Cobb *It's Fun to Write* (Longman 1984) R Philpot *English Handwriting* (Collins 1983) and P Smith and A Inglis *New Nelson Handwriting* (Nelson 1984). The first and last books mentioned provide detailed guidance in the form of teachers' books.
4 The illustrative material in 12.3 (a) comes from *New Nelson Handwriting*. Other illustrations in 12.3 (b) and 12.3.1 are from *It's Fun to Write*.

# Appendix: Cohesive devices

The purpose of this appendix is to provide a more extensive reference list of the rhetorical features discussed in 2.2.2. It is intended to serve as a checklist of items which should gradually be learned in the course of a writing programme going up to the intermediate level. For more complete treatments, see Quirk et al (1972) and Halliday and Hasan (1976).

## A Logical devices

For ease of reference, the logical connectors listed below are given in alphabetical order. Some examples are also provided.

(a) *Addition*

| | | |
|---|---|---|
| again | equally | in fact |
| also | further (more) | moreover |
| and | in addition (to . . .) | too |
| and then | indeed | what is more |
| besides | | |

Examples:

The house faces north, so it never gets the sun. *Also*, it is rather damp.

The children do not like one another. *Moreover*, they often quarrel and start to fight.

She hardly ever goes to the theatre. *In fact*, she has not been for months.

(b) *Comparison*

| | | |
|---|---|---|
| compared with | in the same way | similarly |
| in comparison with | likewise | |

Examples:

I used to work fifteen hours a day. *In comparison with that*, my present job is more like a holiday!

The doctor advised him to give up smoking. *Similarly*, he recommended him to eat much less and take plenty of exercise.

(c) *Contrast and concession**

| | | |
|---|---|---|
| besides | naturally | still |
| but | nevertheless | whereas |
| however | of course | while |
| in contrast | on the contrary | yet |
| instead | on the other hand | |

*Some of these items imply both contrast *and* concession (for example: *however*), while others, such as *on the contrary, on the other hand*, are more clearly concerned with contrastive relationships between sentences. On the whole, however, it seemed more convenient to subsume these items under one heading.

Examples:

He did not show anyone the papers. *Instead*, as soon as he got a chance, he burnt them.

She is not as pretty as she used to be. *Nevertheless*, she is still a very attractive girl.

His first novel took him only a few weeks to write, *while* his next one took over a year.

(d) *Enumeration*

| | | |
|---|---|---|
| first(ly) (second(ly), etc.) | last | on top of (that) |
| finally | next | to (begin with) |
| in the (first) place | more important | then |

Examples:

His job involves a number of things. *First*, he is responsible for general administration in the office. *Secondly*, he has to look after the financial side of the business . . . *Finally*, he has been asked to build up outside contacts.

There were several good reasons for changing the plan. *To begin with*, it involved a lot of money. *On top of that*, it needed too many people.

(e) *Exemplification*

| | |
|---|---|
| as (evidence of . . .) | such as |
| for example | thus |
| for instance | to show what (I mean) |
| let us (take the case of . . .) | |

Examples:

Most countries do not grow enough food for their needs. *Let us take the case of* the United Kingdom.

Most people are superstitious in some way. *Thus*, a lot of people believe that the number 13 is unlucky . . .

(f) *Inference*

| | | |
|---|---|---|
| if not, . . . | otherwise | then |
| in (that) case | that implies | |

Examples:

He left the country the same day. *In that case*, he must have had his passport with him.

You must get some more petrol. *Otherwise*, we will not have enough to get us to the next town.

(g) *Summary*

| | | |
|---|---|---|
| in all | in short | on the whole |
| in brief | in conclusion | to sum up |

Examples:

She spends a lot of money on clothes. She is also fond of buying expensive jewellery. *In short*, she is extremely extravagant.

The car is not new but it is in good condition. The price too is very reasonable. *On the whole*, I think it is quite a good bargain.

The film has a very unusual plot, with plenty of action. Both the acting and photography are excellent. *To sum up*, this is a film you should not miss.

(h) *Time**

| | | |
|---|---|---|
| after (a while) | before (that time) | since (then) |
| afterwards | finally | so far |
| at first | in the end | then |
| at last | meanwhile | (up to) (then) |
| at (the same time) | next | |

Examples:

He tried to open one of the small windows. *At first* it remained firmly closed but, *in the end*, after a great deal of effort, he managed to open it a few inches.

. . . and the fire has finally been brought under control. Several men are still missing. *Meanwhile* the causes of the explosion are still being investigated.

(i) *Result*

| | | |
|---|---|---|
| accordingly | for that reason | then |
| as a result | hence | therefore |
| consequently | the (consequence) of that is . . . | thus |

Examples:

Most people were opposed to the scheme on the grounds that it was too expensive. *Accordingly*, it is now being re-examined to see if costs can be reduced.

Seven inches of snow fell during the night, blocking most main roads. *As a result*, traffic conditions have been chaotic.

In the past, no one has taken his advice very seriously. *Hence*, it is very probable that he will not be inclined to help on this occasion.

(j) *Reformulation*

| | |
|---|---|
| in other words | that is (to say) |
| rather | to put it more (simply) |

Examples:

Towards the end of the party he got up and danced on the table. *In other words*, he made a complete fool of himself.

Most people felt that the project was not worthwhile in proportion to the amount of time it would take to complete it and equally the financial expenditure involved. *To put it more simply*, it was a waste of time and money.

*That is, indicating temporal relationships. This is a very open-ended group of devices, as the number of bracketed items shows. For example, instead of *at the same time*, we may have: *at that time/at that moment*.

(k) *Replacement*

| | | |
|---|---|---|
| again | (better) still | the alternative is . . . |
| alternatively | on the other hand | |

Examples:

It is very likely that we shall go by car, even though it is a long drive, because we shall need some means of transport while we are there. *Alternatively*, we might fly out and hire a car when we arrive.

If things get any worse, we might have to arrange a public meeting to discuss the matter. *Better still*, we could even organise a demonstration.

(l) *Transition*

| | |
|---|---|
| as far as . . . is concerned | now |
| as for . . . | to turn to . . . |
| incidentally | with (reference) to . . . |

Examples:

We can leave most of the details of the proposal until the next meeting. *Now, as far as* money *is concerned*, this needs careful consideration.

In the end, he decided to sell his car. This, *incidentally*, proved to be a mistake.

## B Grammatical and lexical linking devices

In this section there are further examples of the devices referred to in 2.2.2(b) and 2.2.2(c).

(a) *Use of pronominal forms to replace noun phrases*

*Napoleon* was a great soldier. *He* was also a great administrator.

John bought *a new car*. It cost a lot of money, but it goes a lot better than his old *one*.

*John and Mary* are going on holiday to Brazil. *Their* friends are very envious.

He decided to take *some heavy shoes* with him. He thought that *these* would be useful in case he went walking.

(b) *Use of pronominal forms to replace adverbials (noun phrases of time and place)*

He left *the following day*. He knew *then* that he was not coming back.

We called on them *soon after breakfast*. We should have realised that *this* was a bad time for a visit.*

I decided to take my books back to *the library*. When I got *there*, I found it was closed.

*Noun phrases are also used as replacives. For example: John was born *just before the war. At that time* his parents lived in London.

(c) *Use of pronominal forms to replace clauses or sentences*

*Some students work all night just before an exam. This* is a great mistake.

*John has just resigned. It* was quite unexpected.

Notice that in the examples above the pronominal forms all refer back to something previously mentioned. They may also refer forward. For example:

*This* is what you should do. *You should be very frank.*

My advice is *as follows. Be very frank.*

(d) *Use of determiners (the, this, that, etc.) to refer back to a previous noun phrase*

*Thieves* broke into *a* jeweller's *shop* in North Street last night. *The thieves* entered *the shop* through a small back window.

I bought *a pocket calculator* last year. *That calculator* has proved very useful.

*Former* and *latter* are used to refer back to one of two previous noun phrases.

*John and Tom* both took part in the play. Only *the former* has had any real experience of acting. *The latter* had never even been on the stage before.

(e) *Repetition of key words*

These particular train services are not used very much by *commuters*. As a rule, *commuters* tend to travel much earlier.

(f) *Use of synonyms to avoid repetition*

These cars were first *made* in 1972. When they were first *produced*, they were not very popular.

If you have any *thoughts* on the subject, please let me know. I shall be interested to hear your *ideas*.

(g) *Use of a construction implying whole-part or part-whole relationship*

You will need to take some *tools* with you. You can get *a hammer, a saw and a screwdriver* from most big department stores.

*Large cars and lorries* are not advised to use this route. These *vehicles* should take the other road.

(h) *Use of related word forms*

Seven people have been *arrested* so far. The *arrests* were made late last night.

(i) *Use of parallel structures*

*It is possible* that the plan will succeed. *It is* equally *possible* that it will fail.

# Bibliography

ABBOTT, E 'Teaching English Spelling to Adult Beginners' *English Language Teaching Journal* XXXIII:2 1979

ABBOTT, J and WINGARD, P *The Teaching of English as an International Language* (Collins 1981)

ALLEN, H B and CAMPBELL, R N (eds) *Teaching English as a Second Language* (McGraw Hill 1972)

ALLEN, J P B and CORDER, S P (eds) *The Edinburgh Course in Applied Linguistics 3* (Oxford University Press 1974)

ARNOLD, J and HARMER, J *Advanced Writing Skills* (Longman 1978)

BARZUN, J and GRAFF, H F *The Modern Researcher* (Harcourt, Brace and World 1970)

BOUCHARD, D L and SPAVENTA, L J (eds) *A TEFL Anthology* selected articles from *English Teaching Forum* (1980)

BRIERE, E 'Quantity before Quality in Second Language Composition' (*Language Learning* 16:3, 4 1966)

BROUGHTON, G, BRUMFIT, C, FLAVELL, R, HILL, P and PINCAS, A *Teaching English as a Foreign Language* (Routledge and Kegan Paul 1978)

BRUMFIT, C *Communicative Methodology in Language Teaching* (Cambridge University Press 1984)

BYRNE, D *Teaching Oral English* (new edition) (Longman 1986)

BYRNE, D *Focus on the Classroom* (Modern English Publications 1988)

BYRNE, D *Progressive Picture Compositions* (Longman 1967)

BYRNE, D *Just Write*! (Macmillan 1988)

CARRIER, M *Writing* (Hodder and Stoughton 1981)

CLOSE, R A *A Reference Grammar for Students of English* (Longman 1975)

COBB, D *It's Fun To Write* (Longman 1984)

COE, N, RYCROFT, R and ERNEST, P *Writing Skills* (Cambridge University Press 1983)

CROFT, K (ed) *Readings on English as a Second Language* (Winthrop 1980)

DAVIES, A (ed) *Problems of Language and Learning* (Heinemann 1975)

DONLEY, M 'Precis Writing: a Rehabilitation' (*English Language Teaching Journal* XXIX:3 1975)

DOUGHTY, P, PEARCE, J and THORNTON, J *Exploring Language* (Arnold 1972)

DUNN, O *Developing English with Young Learners* (Macmillan 1984)

FLEMING, G *Guided Composition* revised by H J S Taylor (Hodder and Stoughton 1975)

FREEMAN, D *The David Freeman Show* (Modern English Publications 1985)

GLENDINNING, E and MANTELL, H *Write Ideas* (Longman 1981)

HALLIDAY, M A K and HASAN, R *Cohesion in English* (Longman 1976)

HARMER, J *The Practice of English Language Teaching* (Longman 1983)

HEATON, J B *Composition through Pictures* (Longman 1966)

HEATON, J B *Beginning Composition through Pictures* (Longman 1975)

HEATON, J B *Writing through Pictures* (Longman 1986)

HEDGE, T *Pen to Paper* (Nelson 1983a)

HEDGE, T *In a Word* (Nelson 1983b)

HILL, L A *Writing for a Purpose* (Oxford University Press 1978)

HOLDEN, S (ed) *English for Specific Purposes* (Modern English Publications 1977)

HOLDEN, S (ed) *Teaching Children* (Modern English Publications 1980)

HOLDEN, S (ed) *Second Selections from Modern English Teacher* (Longman 1983)

HORN, V 'Using Connectives in Elementary Composition' (*English Language Teaching* XXVI:2 1972)

HUBBARD, P, JONES, H, THORNTON, B and WHEELER, R *A Training Course for TEFL* (Oxford University Press 1983)

JOHNSON, K and MORROW, K (eds) *Communication in the Classroom* (Longman 1981)

JOLLY, D *Writing Tasks* (Cambridge University Press 1984)

JONES, K *Simulations in Language Teaching* (Cambridge University Press 1982)

JUPP, T and MILNE, J *Basic Writing Skills in English* (Heinemann 1980)

KNIGHT, R *Writing 2* (Cassell 1986)

KRASHEN, S *Writing: Research, Theory and Applications* (Pergamon 1984)

LAVER, J and HUTCHESON, S (eds) *Communication in Face to Face Interaction* (Penguin 1972)

MARKSTEIN, L and GRUNBAUM, D *What's the Story?* (Longman 1981)

MATTHEWS, A, SPRATT, M and DANGERFIELD, L (eds) *At the Chalkface* (Arnold 1985)

O'DRISCOLL, J *Advanced Writing Skills* (Penguin 1984)

PAULSTON, C B 'Teaching Writing in the ESOL Classroom' (*TESOL Quarterly* 6:1 1972)

PHILPOT, R *English Handwriting* (Collins 1983)

PINCAS, A *Teaching English Writing* (Macmillan 1982a)

PINCAS, A *Writing in English Books 1–3* (Macmillan 1982b,c 1983)

PULLUM, G P 'Indian Scripts and the Teacher of English' (*English Language Teaching* XXV:3 1971)

QUIRK, R, GREENBAUM, S, LEECH, G and SVARTVIK, J *A Grammar of Contemporary English* (Longman 1972)

RAIMES, A *Techniques for Teaching Writing* (Oxford University Press 1983)

RIDOUT, R *Write Now* (Longman 1975)

SEWARD, B H 'Teaching Cursive Writing to EFL Students' (*English Language Teaching* XXVI:2 1972)

SHARWOOD-SMITH, M 'A Note on "Writing versus Speech"' (*English Language Teaching Journal* XXXI:1 1976)

SMITH, F *Writing and the Writer* (Heinemann 1982)

SMITH, P and INGLIS, A *New Nelson Handwriting* (Nelson 1984)

WATERS, D *Primary School Projects* (Heinemann 1982)

WHITE, R *Teaching Written English* (Heinemann 1980)

WILLIS, J *Teaching English through English* (Longman 1981)

WINGFIELD, R J 'Five Ways of Dealing with Errors in Written Composition' (*English Language Teaching Journal* XXIX:4 1975)

WOODS, L *Writing 1* (Cassell 1986)

ZAMEL, V 'Writing: The Process of Discovering Meaning' (*TESOL Quarterly* 16 1981)

ZAMEL, V 'The Composing Process of Advanced ESL Students: Six Case Histories' (*TESOL Quarterly* 17 1983)

*The Art of TESOL* Selected Articles from English Teaching Forum (1982)

# Index